OUR PORTION

# OUR PORTION

*New and Selected Poems*

Philip Terman

Autumn House Press

PITTSBURGH

*Autumn House Press Staff*

Michael Simms: Founder, Editor-in-Chief, and President
Eva Simms: Co-Founder
Giuliana Certo: Managing Editor
Christine Stroud: Associate Editor
Alison Taverna: Assistant Editor
Ashleigh Fox: Intern
Sharon Dilworth, John Fried: Fiction Editors
J.J. Bosley, CPA: Treasurer
Anne Burnham: Fundraising Consultant
Michael Wurster: Community Outreach Consultant
Jan Beatty: Media Consultant
Heather Cazad: Contest Consultant
Michael Milberger: Tech Crew Chief

Autumn House Press receives state arts funding support through a grant from the Pennsylvania Council on the Arts, a state agency funded by the Commonwealth of Pennsylvania, and the National Endowment for the Arts, a federal agency.

ISBN: 978-1-938769-06-1
Library of Congress Control Number: 2015931288

*For Joseph and Mildred*

*and*

*Chris, Miriam, and Bella*

# CONTENTS

*I carry the synagogue within me.*

—Edmond Jabés

# AMONG THE SCRIBES

*New Poems*

Didn't they tell you, all those sages,
that the promised land is this moment?

Here, now, this late summer air, this dew-drenched field,
this thin filament of gossamer between an apple tree and an apple
    tree?
The almost unnoticeable blue jay feather in the unmown grass?

Remember when you were Moses?
Remember when you couldn't speak
and they spit on you and you garbled and slurred your words?

Always you were singular as the swallowtail
losing itself in the goldenrod profusion.

Remember when you were Whitman?
Twirling a leaf of grass?—like this morning:
coffee, beside your wife,
in the shadow of the shade garden and a sassafras,

drops of tree-rain dripping patterns on your page,
hydrangeas streaked with the pink of their next incarnation,
the children picking pears, filling their baskets with silliness.

History and the future leave you suspended
like a hummingbird's pause.

A leaf falls.
Who ordered these distractions?

The rain tells you one thing, the silence another,
but that traitor, summer, that shameful lover,
gathers back to itself its sweetness, its light, reclaiming its juices,

so you want to sing poems deep
as those psalms chanted with exact pronunciation to the text,
the precise cantillations, the pauses and stresses,
and—beautiful, the way that swallowtail now dips and dives
its yellow into the yellow of the sunflowers.

Are you adding to the law?
Are you composing your holy writ?
Don't we all want to translate each moment into the eternal?

Isn't this your flowering time?
Aren't you robed in royalty?
And shouldn't every word be a fiery contribution?

And aren't even you among the scribes?

# BERNIE COULD HAVE BEEN MY FATHER

Bernie would drive all the way to Youngstown
for a few pounds of corned beef and rye bread,

the kind with seeds we'd consume with onion rings
and Dr. Brown's black cherry soda. He wasn't

my father, but he could have been, I could have
learned my bar mitzvah lesson in the backseat

of his Lincoln Town Car on the way to the track.
I could have witnessed how he'd play the numbers

between customers of L and L Glass and Paint Co.,
in Butler, Pennsylvania, and on the Sabbath,

I could have listened as he chanted
the tropes of the Torah portion, tone deaf but

accurate, holding the synagogue together,
a synagogue himself, if a man could embody

a congregation, and Bernie did, his heart
so devoted to this struggling house of God,

its roof dripping during the difficult part
of the service, the part where you have to stand

and read silently so that only God will hear you—
Bernie had that fixed, too, he had a number to call

out of his infinite list of numbers of plumbers
and painters and general cleaners he'd pay

off the books, this "unofficial mayor of Butler,"
his son—which I could have been—called him,

because he never went anywhere he wasn't known,
even in some roadside diner in South Carolina

someone would be at the next table who'd
recognize him from somewhere, some roulette

wheel in Atlantic City, maybe he saw Bernie
pass out $100 bills to each of his sons

and his sons' friends and to all his grandchildren
and maybe even strangers because Bernie

wanted everyone to have a good time, his body
now lowered into the earth he faithfully mowed

and tended, surrounded by the congregation
he made sure would continue—

and we will continue, Bernie, you can bet on it.

# GARDENER, WHISTLING

Like synagogue singers whose psalms
are never wholly absent from their lips,

the gardener, softly, almost to herself, whistles
her way down the rows as she plants

the corn seeds, whistles watering the tomatoes,
lips puckered in the spontaneous melody

of the moment—whistles studying the poppies,
whistles examining the vines for grapes,

whistles testing the air for rain,
whistles hoeing until dusk turns

to dark, whistles the children to bed,
whistles her calloused feet in the bath,

whistles the robins and mourning doves
who weave her whistle into their song.

ON THE 23RD ANNIVERSARY OF MY FATHER'S
PASSING, I READ "LINES WRITTEN A FEW MILES
ABOVE TINTERN ABBEY" WITH MY DAUGHTER


Corn stubble and stalks freshly plowed,
apples recently fallen in summer's

last wisps of warmth. If I listen
closely, I can still hear you calling

my name for supper—more insistent
each year as with each year

I'm more distracted with my life.
Now, at the table on our porch,

overlooking the harvested garden,
the fallen leaves—a wild, secluded

scene, a Sunday afternoon, surrounded
by woods and copses—no hedgerows,

but in the near distance perhaps
a hermit's cave or two—I assist

my daughter with Wordsworth, puzzling
out this long poem that insists on love

for nature, on *recollection of senses sweet*.
I want her to know that passion,

that *sublime*, a word she looks up
and discovers: "grandeur," "awe," and,

after a bit of struggle, I want her
to understand what *living soul*

might mean, and *seeing into the life
of things*, what these years, your absence,

has taught me—and, perhaps, what mine
might teach her—*that all we behold*—

these cobalt streaks of sky visible
through empty branches, this garden soil

still holding remnants of spring's plantings,
this poetry, *is full of blessings*.

## TEACHING MY DAUGHTER
## THE MOURNER'S KADDISH

Forget the original Aramaic,
or Ezekiel's vision that served

as inspiration. I just hope for the Hebrew,
but she prefers the transliteration—

which, no matter the alphabet, translates
into *magnification* and *sanctification*—

thinking of the story about the rabbi
building a fire in the woods,

and reciting a prayer—and who was the rabbi
and where the woods were located

and how the fire was built were all forgotten,
but not the prayer, never the prayer—child,

this is the one sad song I do not wish you to sing,
elegy of sorrow, gate of grief I would forbid you

to enter, these same syllables mourners
have pronounced for millennia, which I rise

to chant, according to their anniversary,
for my father, my mother, my brother—

the rhythms you will enrich
with each repetition and, soon enough, over

me, so I call your name and instruct:
*chant it again, from the beginning, more slowly.*

# PUTZING AROUND

*after Neruda*

It happens I'm tired of being a Jew.
It happens that I go into synagogues shriveled up.
I stroll around the Jewish Community Center
singing "Hava Nagila" in falsetto.
The smell of my mother's challah makes me sob out loud.
I want nothing but the repose of either barbequed pork or shellfish,
I want to see no more maps of Israel, nor *mezuzahs,*
nor Stars of David, nor fancy kabbbalistic necklaces.
It happens that I'm tired of my facial hair and sideburns.
It happens I'm tired of being a Jew.
Just the same it would be delicious
to scare a wasp with a *yarmulke*
or knock a nun dead with one slap of my *tefillin.*
It would be beautiful
to run naked through the streets with a kosher knife
*kibitzing* until they crucify me.
I do not want to go on being a Talmudic *nudnik,*
*kvetching,* atoning, *davening* in the sanctuary,
standing and sitting, repeating the same words every day.
I don't want to be the inheritor of so much guilt,
as the last denier, a stiff-necked corpse.
For this reason Leviticus infects us all,
with its strictures and its restrictions,
howling its Jehovah.
I want to visit the houses of the gentiles,
certain bakeries smelling of lard,
streets full of *shiksas* begging for my attention.
There are Jewish mothers beckoning from doors
of the houses which I hate,

statues of their adored sons on the suburban lawns,
stuffed ancestors displayed above the couch,
and holy *tchotchkes* from Jerusalem all over the place.
It happens that I'm tired of being a Jew.

*Let's plant a tree on every corner of speech.*

I need to stop writing your words, Sohrab,
or my poems will look exactly like yours—
and my devotion, even in translation,

will get me arrested, as I already am,
for your: *The pure sound of love*
*vaguely shedding its skin.*

See how easily I marry your lines
into mine—Hafez, Rumi, Khayyam:
that Persian tradition,

a whole other script, and all I do is fall
in love with your squiggles and flourishes,
your *wet night of affection*. Aroused,

I have to lay the book aside, storm off,
calm myself in this still-hovering
morning moon, lose myself

beyond the cemetery, the just-plowed
field: the glare, the frost, the fog,
the jewel-glittering dew, wondering:

how many gods are living nearby?
How many birds are singing in my heart?
How many springs did I bargain for?

Genial, courteous, shy, retiring, never
married, living with your mother and sister,
attired in Japanese sandals, casual,

the way your poems can travel comfortably
from one language to another:
*I had never known two poplars to be enemies.*

In order to compose, you needed the space
the earth's canvas could provide,
and the solitude, nothing—no one—

in the way of that lucidity:
*eyes should be washed to see in a different way.*
And it's true: we want our life clarified,

we want our relations to reveal themselves
for what they absolutely are, in all their dark
complexities, their wounds, their terrors.

Sometimes, more than sometimes,
I'm afraid of the world outside of your words
and this notebook, where the narrative

is too much for me, all that long lifetime,
those characters and plots and story arcs
and climaxes and dénouements, all that drama,

all that weight I've been shifting
from shoulder to shoulder. Instead:
*Let's allow solitude to sing* and save

a little time for ourselves, a tree root,
a hay bale where we can retreat, consider,
where the past and future dissolve, not

the grave, where we'll spend time soon
enough, but the size of our shadow,
where only God can find us, far away

from *the tiresome presence of objects*.
In the photo we are only shone
the bottom half of your contemplating body,

your long fingers cupping the pomegranate.
You paid too much attention to the inner life,
they said. You weren't a storyteller, as if

we have to make that kind of sense.
They said you weren't political—you used
too many words too many people could understand.

You praised God too much. Too shy,
you'd skip your own art openings, preferring
the villagers and deserts around Kashan.

Now, I'm eating an orange in the sunlight,
or the sun in an orange light, tasting the truth of this
juice-on-the-tongue, like reading you, each

succulent word, savoring the rest of my life
by saying your tropes to everyone I meet, neglecting
to give you credit, because you're the poet

I want to be, as in: *which road will take me*
*to the garden of distances?* Or: *I saw daylight*
*fluttering in a doorless cage*.

I can't help this, Sohrab. I turn to you so often
I have to make a public display of it.
Someone get me a spray can. Someone

find me an abandoned building with blank walls
so I can inscribe in my illegible script: *and the mind
fanned itself with the luminous surface of a flower*—

or weave my words into the water of your words,
or visa versa—*it would be a good thing*, we say,
*if the seeds of a person's heart were visible*

*as the pomegranate seeds* and I'm nodding
to the rhythm of the neighbor's cow mooing
its one song: one must be a source and a way

to a source. One must come upon a place
where one can say: why should I leave this place?
One could do worse than spend a spring evening

with you, after supper, the light lingering,
the sweet scents of lilacs signaling the summer air
to slow down its eternities. Sohrab,

you write my secret book I hide
from everyone, yet I read it everyday
when I am most alone, most alone, and in love.

# WITH MY BROTHER AT WALDEN POND

*for David Terman*

Twilight, January air unseasonably warm,
we add our stones to the pile that was

his house. Further on, at its reproduction,
we look through a window, imagine Henry

reading the Vedas, chuckling to the sparrow,
minding not the hours. Briefly we balance

the rails where he heard the train's whistle
and said it will ride the backs of the laborers.

And if he heard the power saws and backhoes
clearing and layering the private property

across the road for condominiums? Earlier,
on Poet's Ridge, I tried to be quietly desperate,

to not keep pace with my companion,
my brother the mathematician explaining

the Theory of the Steady State, about how
a system's recently observed behavior

continues into the future.
Thoreau, too, had a brother.

They traveled rivers together.
When he came down, suddenly,

with lockjaw, Henry nursed him
but he died in his arms anyway and Henry

loved him so much he completely lost interest
in nature. He became, he said, "denaturalized."

He loved him so much—this rugged individualist,
this stone cold solitary, this disobedient,

this misanthrope, this independent, who wanted
only trees for company, this loner about whom

Emerson said, "when you touched him, he felt like bark,"
that he developed lockjaw himself, sympathetically.

In the blurred light of this new dark,
either a thin pine leans across the surface

or Henry is a-fishing. Why not?
Behavior continuing into the future.

Henry bragged like Chanticleer, standing on his roost,
to wake his neighbors up. I tried to wake

my brother up once. The younger, I splashed
ice water on his face so he'd rise and toss

the football. He beat the deserved crap
out of me instead. Now we look for stones

flat enough to skip, a skill at which he's
proficient, the advantage of a life of absolute

concentration. Sidearming an obscure slab
he had to scrape for in the hard soil that—why

not?—Henry sparked for his reading lamp,
we follow its hops and circles and widening

undulations, like the motions of the planets,
or our souls rippling back round to water.

*1: At Whitman's House, Camden, New Jersey*

Well, I saw your boot-soles beneath the rocking chair
in the second story bedroom you died in—
you were not contained between them
and your hat, which hung on a peg on a wall,
nor did the bed hold you, or your walking cane
prop you up—you were not contained anywhere
in that house across the street from the prison
whose residents you would celebrate, nor
in the backyard where the vine still spins around
the doorframe, nor in the traffic from the freeway
just beyond the city limits—no, Walt, and I did,
in fact, look for you under those boot-soles,
which were ready and waiting for a pair of feet
to slip into them, and the cane stared back at me with longing.


*2: Reading Whitman to a Friend Who Is Dying*

Hard to find a poem without death in it,
so I pick the one about friendship—

about how to be with those we like is enough—
and I look up at her stretched out on the couch

her husband carried her to after she fainted
when he lifted her out of the hot bath, her limbs

thin as willow vines the leaves are revealing,
her tender skin like a worn sheet, her skull scarred

from the surgery, her blind eye lifted up,
and I say something about *the contact and odor*

*that pleases the soul well*, and then the silence,
and I think perhaps she hasn't heard, or that,

in fact—she is so still—she's passed, and I ask
if she would like to hear another poem—

and, as if from another world, a distinct *yes*—
and I leaf for the exact words that will save her.

CANINE BUDDHA

In losing a dog we lose the era that included the dog.
She accompanied our walks everywhere, traipsing
through the cemetery and across the field—leash-less,

always leash-less, taking off at first deer whiff—chowhound,
insatiable four-legged Whitman, who'd roll her
100 pound beast around and around the skunk-stink—

who wouldn't bathe, who'd scram under the porch
at the sight of a hose, but nevertheless condescended
to dog-paddle after the frisbee we'd toss across the pond,

waddling like a hippo. After long evenings of hide-
and-seek and chasing our bicycle tires as if they were
round rubber rabbits—she'd *plotz* in the middle

of the living room and become a large pillow
for anyone—even me, with my own heaviness, to plop
their head down on that enormous belly and feel

something like the weight of the earth breathing
like an enlightened canine Buddha. But smart
we were not to go near her dinner bowl when

she *fressed*—yes, she was enamored with chewing—
sticks, even rocks her teeth would wear away into dust:
once, she swallowed three twenty dollar bills

and we chalked it up to her insatiability. Near the end,
the tumor spread and the wound enlarged and
she had to wear one of those e-collars so she wouldn't

work her stitches with her teeth and tongue. We didn't
need the veterinarian to tell us she'd never make it
as a three-legged dog. Gentle animal, you were never trivial.

Only scientists could figure out a way to reduce
your colossal presence into our tin container—
so we could—what, with your bulk we'd never consider—

lift you up and scatter you into every surrounding scent.

Because the synagogue pipes burst
in the coldest part of the winter,
causing mildew in the holy ark, the Torah

became damp, edges curled like dried
leaves, stitched sinews loosened
between sheets of sheepskin, dabs of ink—

prepared ages ago from soot, tree sap
and honey, dissolved in gallnut juice, scribed
with the feather of a goose, its quill

a reed and not a weapon of destruction—
bleeding through the parchment.
And the two women lift its heaviness,

delicately remove the silver crown
and breastplate, unfasten its pointer,
slip off the velvet robe,  unscroll

and spread out all five books across
the length of the sanctuary, 304,
805 letters exposed and revealed

to the open air, from *In the beginning*
to the death of Moses, *whom the Lord knew
face to face.* They press their own faces

close to the surface as they can, closer,
without breaking the law of touching it,
inhale deeply the animal flesh: *smells*

*like my horse,* says one. *Like soil,* says
the other. They whisper how it will lay there
overnight in the sanctuary, freed finally

from its closet where it is condemned
to straighten up at attention until
the curtain parts and the congregation

rises—and for once it will be free
from all that worship, all that praise,
all that chanting and bowing and chanting

and bowing. Alone in the silent dark
of its healing, will it remember when
it was torn and spit upon? Will it recall

when it was set on fire? Or will it dream
of all those lovers embracing its body as if
they were quivering on a tottering earth

all the days and nights of their lives?

# I'M THE SAME AGE AS JAMES WRIGHT WHEN HE DIED

Difficult to believe, wise as his poems are,
especially the late ones, the ones in *This Journey*,
the ones of keen observation and calmness,
of trips with his beloved through the great
beautiful places, the ruins of Rome, the statues
of Apollo and Diana, but especially the lizard,
the red-tailed hawk, the grapes his lover picked,
and Ohio, always Ohio, that land of childhood
and heartbreak, which, like the sumac branch,
*more rooted to the tree than the tree is to the ground,*
he could never shake off, that curse, that blessing—
the same age, though to read *This Journey* is to sense
he was an old man, a forefather, an ancient, the sun
suddenly illuminating the spider's web, the years.

Abraham's breaking of the idols is one of my earliest stories,
and I imagined not the act of destruction, but the way
he climbed up on the roof all by himself and looked up at the sky
and imagined how it was all one thing—the stars, his thoughts,
even the pieces of the stone sculptures he smashed, even
his anger at his father for sculpting them, the way I was angry
at my father for the way he'd sip his coffee and lean against
the sink before driving off to the work he hated so that I could
one day grow up and imagine Abraham inventing a religion
that included a father's obligations for his son. Now
it's the Sabbath, another result of that imagined imagining,
and my own child is sifting sand from sand on a summer morning
so indescribably beautiful you can't help but grieve.
The shadowed wings of a turkey buzzard ascend the oaks and maples.
I heard that tale about Abraham in Sunday school.
I don't remember the weather—spring or fall—only that
Abraham was just my age, and now my daughter's,
hiding from his punishment, but, nevertheless, listening.

# OUR SACRIFICE

Daughters, if a crazy, wild voice spoke
in some forsaken place and bid us
to sacrifice you as a test of our faith,
the same wild voice who promised
to make our name, and therefore
your names, great, who would bless those
who would bless us, who would curse
those who would curse us, that voice
that gave us, and therefore you,
this house, these parcels of land—
that same voice that bade us to count
the stars and the sand and spoke
the words: *covenant* and *exceedingly
many*—daughters, even if it means our names
never change, and kings and queens
never go out from us, even if it means
the voice that spoke to us will no longer
speak to us, even if it means the loss
of thousands of years of holiness,
of great structures and stories, of laws
indelible, of rituals enriched
with repetition, even if it means
the abandonment of a people stubborn
and tenacious as the earth itself—
we would not take you—our daughters,
our only daughters—children
of our old age, who gave us laughter—
we would not go up together,
we would not take the wood and knife,
we would not build the fire,

we would not stretch out our hands—
though we would be written out of the book,
though in our refusal we would lose a nation.

## SPRING LEXICON

Two robins in the churchyard are loving it up,
wings treading, spinning around the steeple—
in this first real dusk of spring,

then returning to earth, constructing
their small bowl of shelter.

Don't they know they are on sacred ground?
That just a few feet beyond, a choir is chorusing against the body?

Yet they continue, now swooping and soaring above the cemetery,
beyond our theology, singing.

                    *

Season of coltsfoot and intermittent winds,
of mid-morning snow showers

then quick sun, season of shadows and tools,
of rubber boots, tiny plants under grow lights,

of the cardinal's on again off again affair with our bedroom window,
of red hollyhocks, soft pink poppies, peach honeysuckle, purple clematis,
of pea-sized grapes, of grape-sized apples—

sails of the swallowtail, sighs of the retriever,
a distant hammering under the patriarchal pine,

of leaves lush and cobalt-blue sky-patches
through branch-openings, of windy occasions,

here we can announce that our birth and death are elsewhere,
out there with the out there,
or so far deep inside us they root us to this place and time—

*

A child,
I stood beneath petals
shaped like tiny palms fanning the air
and wondered how those robins concealed themselves in all that daylight.

I climbed the backyard apple tree, its fruit lit from their inside out
to see if I could pet a bird.

I wanted to be so close
I could stroke an orange-reddish breast
or throat, white, streaked with black,

and stare deep into eyes spotted
as the grass and reeds and mud they nest in.

Higher and higher
my thin limbs straddled its limbs
until, at the point I'd have to think my way down,

I caught,
in the hollow where trunk smoothes into branch,
two so wrapped in each others' wings

they couldn't fly away.

*

Sunday night, children put to bed, our bodies in the bath,
between happiness and the rest of the week—

all day we've cleared the ground, gathered branches,
raked leaves, burned them in the center of the garden—

and if this is what we are in the end,
then shouldn't we bring all of ourselves, including our shadows,

into the rhythm, the new arbor, the clematis, the climbing rose:
we dig postholes, we balance and measure, we set concrete and hope it
    stays—

don't tell me this was foreordained,
don't tell me we've been going through the same motion,
a wheel spinning in its recurrence.

It's the sparrow in the about-to-burst lilac,
those indeterminate robins in the tip-top of the apple tree—

the world, a place to start,
the light insisting on its moment, the wind brushing the fallen blossoms
across the shadows of the tree they float from,

and, ahead, all that bird love.

What is the sparrow on the tassels establishing?
Like happiness: here, gone.

Saturday morning, August, pleasure of poetry
and just-picked tomatoes and fresh eggs from the Stallard's chickens.

Meanwhile, the baler scripts its stanzas:
poetry of sweetness,
poetry of all day labor,
poetry the cows will eat.

It's Sabbath: when we pass from the workaday world
and into the world set aside for beauty,
when god collapses in his chair
and lights the candles and blesses himself.

So what if our ancestors were herring dealers
and Talmudic scholars?

*Half of me is dust*, one of them said,
*half of me is wind.*

Even Spinoza, in a less rational mood, inclines to let it go,
let his philosophy of ethics drift off like sleep,
like the crickets in the sassafras,
because certain matters can only be taught in a whisper,
like late summer, this wheel, this parable, this radiance.

Why not a little shade?
Why not slip off our sandals
and soak our calloused feet in the water?

Even the swallowtail rests on the Queen Anne's lace.
Even the koi settle in the shade of the pier.
Even the chicory is shy
in the rarity of its blue.

Afternoons we turn over compost,
shovel thick black soil into the wheelbarrow,
mix it in under the blueberry bushes, rest

and read about the world to come.

And for this little while we believe
in the stillness of the moment,
as if the grapes weren't fattening toward ripeness,

and won't be picked and eaten,
and our children will never grow old.

*Shut up and listen to the music,*
I want to tell this former grand
exalted master but she's sweet,

smiling and chatting us up about
how they serve the best chicken
wings in town on Wednesday nights

and on Mondays it's tacos,
shouting above the high decibel
sliding-like-a-snake-electric six-

string Max Schang screeches
on the small stage, backed only
by Ray Hanna's steady bass and

Steve McMurrey's pounding snares—
Hendrix resurrected at the corner
of 13th and Liberty, Franklin, PA,

Friday night—teachers and respectable
workers from the Joy plant, even
the county commissioner sipping beer,

relaxing awhile in this private club
with "Smoking Permitted" signs,
this weekend retreat where members

can gamble and order shots
of vodka on the honor system—
and now the former exalted master

sways back toward the bar
to the vibrating rhythms Max taunts
all these old-timers with, his axe now behind his back:

*I'm a voodoo chile*, he swears
into the mic: *a vooodooo chile!*
and we're all attention—

it's almost ten o'clock and we know
this is it, the encore, the night's
last number, we're past our bedtime,

when—suddenly, as we reach
for our coats and consider
the long dark walk home, Max

pumps out the first familiar chords
of "All Along the Watchtower,"
and we're not going home yet,

not quite yet.

Remember the summer you read Proust?
In the hammock tied to the apple trees
your daughters climbed, their shadows
merging with the shadows of the leaves
spilling onto those long arduous sentences,
all afternoon and into the evening—robins,
jays, the distant dog, the occasional swaying,
the way the hours rocked back and forth,
that gigantic book holding you in its woven nest—
you couldn't get enough pages, you wished
that with every turning a thousand were added,
the words falling you into sleep, the sleep
waking you into words, the summer you read
Proust, which lasted the rest of your life.

*1. The Former Jewish Quarter in Seville*

"I wish I could show you more,"
Moises says as he walks me
to a far corner of the Alcazar courtyard,

through a narrow opening,
and we arrive on the uneven cobblestones
of the Barrio of Santa Cruz,

the *Juderia*—the Jewish Quarter—
"the *former* Jewish Quarter," Moises emphasizes—
"I don't show you what isn't there:

the kosher butcher, the *mikveh,*
the synagogue where I'd introduce you
to the rabbi and we would *daven* together

and chant *Lecha Dodi*
in our strange Sephardic melodies."
Instead, we pass through La Carne Gate,

walk past the busy Plaza Saint Maria Blanco
where tourists sip espressos
and he shows me remnants of the wall

Alphonso X built for the Jews
"for their own protection. Evidence
claims they'd been here since the 3rd Century,

though legend insists they arrived
before the crucifixion so they wouldn't be blamed
and they'd point, even further back,

to the Book of Obediah, which states:
*. . . and the captivity of Jerusalem which is in Sepharad.*"
We proceed through narrow alleys

shaded by fully-fruited orange trees,
past the open-roofed patios,
the gardens behind fences, pausing

at the only remaining former synagogue
become a church become a hospital
become a church again, which I duly photograph.

We stop at Susona Street, named
for the beautiful Jewess whose love
for a gentile inspired her to confess

her father's plot against the inquisitors,
and so he was caught and burned
at the stake at Spain's first auto-de-fè:

"act of faith," Moises explains.
"In 1481 Susona joined a nunnery, and,
hearing the wails of her father

through the fiery discourses of the Friar,
willed that after her death her skull
be hung above her front door—

and so it was, for a hundred years."
He probes: "Can you still hear them?
The 700 men, women, and children,

forced to eat pork?" And do I also hear
the thousands of peasants gathering,
as if for a fiesta, in this very plaza,

insulting the accused *conversos* wearing
the *sambenito*, the hooded cloak,
decorated with devils thrust into flames of hell?

And who wouldn't, bound to the pyre,
say they would convert? Would I? "How much
does it mean to you? That God?

Today, there are only a few left—
it's not easy to keep the laws.
I get my meat from Madrid."

He shrugs. "One last thing."
We walk toward steps leading underground—
Moises puts his fingers to his lips,

as if not to disturb something,
descending into the dark—
a parking garage, lined with Citroens,

BMWs, Peugeots—packed
in their paid spaces—Moises
squiggles in front of a white van

and points to the wall: a display case,
lit up: inside, a single tomb
of ancient stone—"when they dug the ground

for this garage, they came across—
a cemetery—244 Jewish graves.
They preserved only this one,

and continued digging.
The Muslims have their mosques,
the Christians their cathedrals.

And we Jews? This one tomb,
in an underground garage.
I wish," he whispers, as we ascend the stairs:

"I could have shown you more."


## 2. Yehuda Halevi's Journey to the Promised Land

In Toledo we sat at a small round table
beside a rose garden and the synagogue,
our children grouchy from the long walk and the heat—

I wanted to bump into your ghost
as you chanted that your heart was in the east.
I wanted to hear your songs of praise,

drinking wine with the Arab poets, composing
on the spot, a call and response—
after all, it was the Golden Age,

still a few centuries before the signed order
and the gate closed. So let's quaff
the grape's blood, let's uncage the stag of love,

weave our names into our lines that sing
of this longing to journey, against advice,
to the mystery and the footstool of God,

the law and its fulfillment, the promised land.
From the Cairo Genizah we know your whereabouts,
or most of them, because Jewish law forbids

destruction of any document with God's name,
and everything you wrote had God's name.
You made it to Egypt, but in Fustat

you went back to your old carousing,
writing poems celebrating lutes and dancers,
their ankle bracelets and their black hair:

*I would fall for them all*, you chanted
at the poetry contest, *for their perilous red mouths.*
*For their silver bells of apples and pomegranates.*

How could you put the world behind you
when you were still in love with it?
Yehuda, we journeyed to the plaza named for you

and for a few Euros ordered espressos
and fantas and inquired of someone—anyone—
how far the empty synagogue?

Why does this Jewish Quarter have no Jews?
*Let's have more lutes*, you commanded:
*The foolish heart forgets how old it is.*

Finally you sold your expensive turban,
left Egypt in a rough boat, and sailed
into the hands of God. You stole into

the storehouse of poetry, crept inside
and sealed the door, turning into legend.
Did you touch foot on that elusive soil?

Did you bow down at the Wall?
Or did you die in your desire?
Don't fear, Yehuda. Over the years

your poems became prayers we sing
in the synagogue, as the Torah is lifted,
as the congregation rises, chanted

on the day of mourning, the day
we remember not one but two temples
destroyed, Jerusalem laid to waste,

the people dispersed. Your love poems,
it's true, were made of dew and fire,
but your real instrument was your soul,

which you strummed sweetly, like a harp,
like this warm wind breezing through these roses—
our small portion of paradise, even in this exile.


*3. On a Summer Evening in Western Pennsylvania,
I Struggle With Maimonides'* Guide to the Perplexed

I'm trying to find my way into you, Famous Doctor,
but it's like trying to describe the snow-capped Sierra
Nevada Mountains we drove through on the way

to Cordoba, it's like trying to comprehend the Alhambra
from the perspective of one of those gypsy caves
perched on the other side of the valley—impossible

to take it all in, your life, your works. No fanatic,
you understood the middle path, balancing faith
with reason. I'm trying to read you, Prince of our People,

but the hay baler is rumbling through the field,
lifting the stocky bales for the cows, and here you are,
talking about how, *in the Messianic age,*

*there will be more time for study,* and I wonder—
examining your book on this shadowed porch,
soft breeze quivering the rhododendrons,

newly hatched robins whistling through the afternoon—
isn't this, too, some kind of bliss? That the Messiah
would come—you were convinced, though, you added,

not in your lifetime, but, really, wasn't it because
you wanted us to understand there would be an end
to this misery? Rambam—can I call you that now?—

I wish you could join me, overlooking the garden,
the spring evening in this time of roses and irises,
of mowers and children out of school, in this soft air,

and note the blossoms on the grapes and the blueberries,
listen to the mourning dove's sad five note song,
observe the unexpected nests and know no desire

but what the earth desires in this smeared evening light,
breathe in the intoxication of what the wet earth brings.
You wanted to prove the incorporeality of God.

You wanted your book to guide us through the thickets of the law.
You believed that to heal the body is to heal the soul.
And so: coffee, your book, June, still dew-drenched,

the mock-orange still in its white bloom, and now
six deer leap on the far edge of the adjacent woods
into the almost nothing, an empty field, yet full

of my own ignorance, full of the grasses I can't name,
full of the precise wildflowers and spider webs,
of empty spaces with secrets and infinite goings-on.

In Cordoba they make a big deal of you, your sculpture
in the square near the only remaining synagogue—sitting
on the white chair, holding your book that the fanatics, because

reason was too much for them, burned, whispering
your name to the inquisitors.  But it's still available
in the shops beside reproductions of your statue,

one of which my daughter bought me and stares back
now from beside a vase of orange and yellow lilies.
If, as legend says, I touch your left toe, will I gain

each year in wisdom? Certainly not the learning
you amassed—doctor, rationalist, compiler, rabbi—
bearded, turbaned copper figure sitting, back straight,

right hand clasping your book as if, like the eagle
you were compared to, measuring the Biblical flights,
your left hand clasping the arm of the chair as if holding

yourself to this place, where you knew you were necessary.
And though you did not approve of extravagant praise,
I prefer to be misguided, happily perplexed, in the breeze

of this summer evening, sipping wine, which, you wrote,
is good for me, that it is most exquisite of all nourishments,
how it sustains and encourages the digestive process.

*4. From Spinoza's* Book of God

My mother took these books out
of the Park Synagogue library
and never returned them, these books

on Halevi and Maimonides and Spinoza
and the secret Jews, she snuck them out
the way she'd wrap dinner rolls in napkins

and secure them in her large black purse.
And so I'm writing about these Jews
she'd want me to honor, though

when I was thirteen I sat and stood and sat
and stood beside her during the service,
and suddenly turned to her and said:

"I don't believe this." Did she imagine
that nearly half-a-century later, I'd struggle,
late summer morning, under a glassy sky,

with you, Benito, though I'd rather call you *Baruch*,
another non-believer, who, in your *Book of God*,
say that the more we know God the more we love Him,

and how it's all about essence, and He
doesn't live in the synagogue:
somewhere else, out there: in the earth,

somewhere else, in here: the soul.
*I don't believe this*, we both declared,
for which I received a sideways squint

and you got excommunicated,
though clearly we believe in something,
clearly there's a perfection somewhere—

the absolute stillness of this early afternoon,
deepening in its mixture of shadowed light.
*God,* you said, *like Nature, is infinite.*

There's a slight quivering of honeysuckle,
an afternoon, perhaps, like the one
on July 27, 1656 when you were damned

by a proclamation signed by your own people:
*In accordance with the decisions
of the angels and the saints,*

*with the approval of the holy God
and the entire congregation.* A child,
as you mastered Torah and Talmud,

you heard the auto-de-fè screaming
through your window. So to your own mind you submitted,
excommunicating yourself before they could excommunicate you.

As for me, to my mother I paraphrased Dickinson:
"Some keep the Sabbath by going to Synagogue—
I keep it, staying at Home."

But she didn't command me out of her presence,
she didn't denounce me to the congregation,
she didn't, before God, declare:

*Cursed be he during the day and cursed be he during the night.*
Instead she gave me these secret books
and the memory of her hidden bread:

"Because you never know," she'd whisper.
"You never know when you'll be on your own."
You preferred grinding glass, the clear, fine dust,

a bedstead, an old Turkish robe, a few pair of socks
in need of mending: no stone, no marker,
just your one hundred and eleven books arguing

what the prophets claimed: that to know God
it is impossible not to love God—
you renegade, you defector, you transgressor, you Jew.

"The greatest evil is when you forget that you are the
son of a king."

—Martin Buber, *Tales of the Hasidism*


Yet, aren't I the son of Joe Terman, used car salesman?

And wasn't he the son of Abraham Terman, carpenter,
until injured by a salami truck, or was it a cable car,
on Cedar Hill in Cleveland Heights, Ohio?

And wasn't he the son of—whom?
And how far back do we search for our royalty?

Because my father was not robed but robbed,
and shot in the lower intestine, and pistol whipped.

And if he were a king,
would he have lain on the couch all day,
after they raised the rent, and wept?

And if he were a king, would he have taken
that suited stranger's advice and got himself
some advertising? "Get yourself some advertising,"
he told my father. "Ain't no one gonna know you're here."

"I'll think about it," my father replied,
and showed him the door.

Joe Terman, if you weren't a king, perhaps
you were one of the thirty-six wise peasants,
concealing, beneath your sweater and plaid pants, your esoterica.

Perhaps, between customers, you were studying
Kabbalah and the Zohar in secret.

Did you, in the bathroom where the bodyman stored his *Playboys,*
don your *tefillin* and *yarmulke* and sway to the psalms?

In your filing cabinets, where the title of cars
were kept, just there, did you house your Talmud?

Now that your life has completed itself, Joe
Terman, measured its time and distance,

sung its chapter and verse, and we can look up
every moment of those sixty-seven years,
will we uncover your scepter and crown?

Examining in the minutest detail your errors and triumphs,
will the ornaments of your authority be revealed?

Dusk, the child on the shoulders, tramping
across the field of daisies to the pond where
we toss stale bread to the koi—we crouch

on the dock and watch orange shards of light—
she reads to them aloud, her voice soft,
interweaving with the crickets and the full moon,

frogs croaking beneath the shadowed shore.
Or mornings waiting for the bus, tossing
the football on the driveway, sun just up,

the spiraling pigskin floating between us,
between childhood and adulthood, between
one millennium and another—such a long toss—

between earth and sky, between her life and
my death, back and forth, between it-seems-
like-forever and it-went-by-so-quickly. How

many lifetimes are required to become learned?
Hours unable to slow down heartbeats, when
the last of daylight emerges with glimmerings

of star-rise, when she drops off as over a cliff
into her private world of sleep. Would we trade
forgotten days for one remembered hour?

Can we look deeper into the garment
of the moment? I want both testaments,
the laws and the love, the Patriarchs

and the forgiveness, the psalms and the epistles,
the silence Buddha taught, the Dharma
and the java, the vegetable love and the rebirth,

the apples, released, singing: *August,* singing
*harvest,* singing *only now*, singing *only here.*
Remember those two horses grazing the corner field?

I'd slow and stop and we'd roll down the windows
and stare into their faces, and we named them:
hers was Franny and mine was Bud because

they were the two we rode through the orchard,
me on Bud and her on Franny, led by Autumn,
the college student, and the next time we visited

they were all gone—Franny and Bud and Autumn,
even the apple trees were stripped, and so we pretend
these two stallions are those same two, and imagine

Autumn somewhere in the house beyond,
stepping outside with her riding boots and smile,
the one she wore when we knew her. Or

the fireworks, the thundering booms trickling
their colors and she asks where they come from—
the green and the pink, the blue and the red,

and I wish I could tell her where everything
comes from—that moment of lit-up explosions
and how the streaks linger through the starry dark

until they disappear. When the orphanage director
handed her to me, and I gathered her to my chest,
her piercing scream like an opening of a wound,

and we knew, though at a level deep as where water
cools, that our lives were turning into some new thing,
as if we suddenly grew wings, something unreal

and certain like that, our bodies introduced to this
other body we'll know as our own. Each day
we walk the gravel path around the cemetery,

playing hide-and-seek, she hiding behind a stone,
me pretending I don't find her, though the dog does.
This moment, this thin surface of water.

She chases fireflies across the dusky air.
You, too, were a child, remember?
You, too, lived forever.

Though we didn't know it at the time,
the purpose of the walk was the bluebird.

Hiking for first signs of spring—
the swampy skunk cabbage,
mayflowers' green umbrellas,

imagining trilliums' three petals,
white or pink, imagining
Jack-in-the-pulpits and Georgia O'Keefe

—these few hours of early spring—
imagining the dogwood's white brevities,

and—in a patch of woods,
in the center of everything—a blossom, blue—

and I called your name:
it waited, you looked up, then it flew off—

　　　　*

God kissed me and gave me breath.
You kissed me and took it away.

All we ask for is time—more of it,
we're greedy for it—we skipped work
and crossed Sandy Creek, we took
advantage of the one day of sunlight—

what is this thing, this being alive
and well, why has this happiness arrived

and stayed, what are these gifts of hours
tumbling as if out of some exhausted cloud—

these hours we fritter away,
waiting for the school bus, our days revolving

the way the world spins to a child,
who's just spun senselessly because she is a child?

*

*It's already a song*, says the robin in the hydrangea.

*Or a sweet odor*, says the Madonna lily to the crowd of bee balm.

*Or a softening of the air*, says the yellow swallowtail.

*Or a dusking of the light*, says the unfathomable sky.

Where will the butterfly lean our attention
as it skitters lightly
across the tip-tops of the cornstalks?

And how are journeys determined,
destination by destination?

And how is it possible to forget about the dead,
negligent creatures that we are,

the way a loved one disappears into a distance
we are incapable of distinguishing?

*

The world acquires flavor only when a little
of the other world is mingled into it,

like the blue jay in the blueberry bush:
flapping its wings, screeching to be freed

from the black netting secured with wooden
clothes pins—when I approached
with my copper pot and visions of pie à la mode,

I knew it was my task to release him,
ashamed as he was, shrieking from one end
of the bush to the other, feathers floating.

I unpinned the netting, carefully,
turned it over, silently spoke the bird
toward the opening, though it lingered . . .

sacrificing the sky for its hunger.

                    *

So the most proper study
is outdoors: the hummingbird dipping

its needle beak into the open mouth
of the morning glory, the retriever

dashing off in a flash and rolling in the scent
of a dead skunk: if I could follow through
like that—the way she burrows into a deer's

abandoned rib cage, whittling the bones down
all afternoon and into the evening. She knows
the wisdom of the masters, but I flounder,

following the forms of dailiness: coffee
and paper, breakfast and school bus, the long arc

of work, supper, a situation comedy, and,
after the children sleep, thick novels, longing.

                    *

Did you study the wisdoms?
Was your business honorable?

That's what will be required of you.

Did you sing
your portion of sunlight,
of looking through windows
mornings-into-afternoons,

the whole day yours,
spreading itself into evening,
and suddenly—
the music of crickets,

a hummingbird's worth of air,

the portion you were allotted,
the dust-mote of your existence?

                    *

So if it all depends on the miraculous—
blue jay shrieking from the cornstalks,
woodpecker nose-diving into the spruce,

small maple leaf tossed onto my notebook,
for luck, I hope, for long life and love,
thinking this page is the earth, that in time

it will turn into soil and grow back again,
half in shadow, half in light—must one
abandon one's affairs and enter into

the garden's palace?

Solomon ibn Gabirol, Sephardic sage,
said he spent his life searching for truth
while others have wasted their substance

on love,  the way—let's confess:

                         *

we bite into our hours,
chew the minutes, swallow the seconds,

because the willow knows its secret
but isn't telling
and the grapevine doesn't hesitate to expand itself.

And in the wind's book, we read:
*Remember your fate,*
the one about *that's all she wrote.*

Call it the dream or the carrying forth,
call it the seasonal reach, edgeless, gathering and feasting,
touching awhile, by accident or grace,

call it our portion—

We are not nothing.
We are transmigratory souls.

Pedometer attached to her belt, your mother, spry and strong
at eighty, joins the other Methodist Church members
in calculating the 5,915 miles, no matter the weather, to add up
all the way from Linesville, Pennsylvania to Jerusalem.
They need not worry about miracles or pausing
at the signs of the cross. They need not stop for security
to check their purses for weapons. They need no visa
nor baggage, no money to exchange for shekels, no guide-
book, no guide. They need no ancient tongue or prophecies.
They are, simply, day by day, walking, mile after mile:
the sink to the table, uptown to the post office, down
the block to visit the sick neighbor.  Sundays to and from church.
And when they walk far enough, adding up their pedometers
together, they will arrive in Jerusalem. And keep walking.

*from* THE HOUSE OF SAGES

*1. One Day This Will All Be Yours*

*I don't fall in love*
*with any of them,* my father says,
his back hunched
over the titles on his desk,
the butt-end of the cigar

he can't smoke at home
torn as a crumbled dollar bill.
During the riots
the place was torched,
the neighborhood clogged

like arteries
in the year of the heart attack.
Now, pennants hanging from wires
in rows above the cars
cough dust into Cleveland humidity.

My father tells me to wash
the front line, claims
I think manual labor
is a Mexican. A customer arrives,
looks over a brown Dodge.

*It's good transportation*, he says.
He sold one without an engine once.
I hose a hood clean
of pollution
that splotches everywhere.

Back in the office,
over gin rummy,
my father sweeps his eyes
over his rented property:
*Son, one day this will all be yours.*
He picks up the gut card

I throw him, places it gently
into his spread, slides it down
with his elbow, pauses,
and gins.
*Didn't I tell you never to speculate?*


## 2. *Our Only Guarantee*

The cars face Euclid Avenue
in uneven rows,
wise in their junk frames.

The bodyman wheels them in,
removes rust, spray paints,
assigns each a place:

in front—'68 Pontiac,
'73 Olds, '66 Caddy,
pink, with A.C.,

'80 Mustang with music,
in back—the junkers
that won't turn over,

weeds jetting out of fenders,
hoods, trunks, doors open to give
one more spare part: jack and hubcap,

radiator and radio.
Each is priced: *As Is.*
Our only guarantee is to the curb.

Used and sold, used and sold,
spun down countless highways,
driven beyond their limits,

stalled, abandoned
just after the breakdowns,
how did they congregate

in this gravel yard
like pilgrims gathered
at the holy land?


*3. The Last of the Hippies*

Jesse the bodyman, a pimp on the side, makes the cars hum, in the
greasy garage, windowless, tires stacked to the tilting point, country
music blasting from the transistor, the toilet backed up, *Playboy*
centerfolds shaping the dust, tools haphazard on the cracked-cement
floor.

"Get you any woman you want," he says, but, seventeen, I sneak
phone calls to my girlfriend or lie on the black vinyl couch reading *The
Brothers Karamozov*, my father shuffling through car titles on his desk:
"Go watch Jesse," he'd say. "You might learn something."

Having business at the bank, he puts me in charge, shows me a list
with two columns scrawled in pencil, one marked "preferred price" and
the other "lowest we'll go."

"Back in a few minutes," and no sooner he's out the door, he pauses:
"If you get any customers, try to hold them until I get back. Stall them—
show them around, start a few cars."

Humid afternoon, air all haze, trash stench from the next door's McDonald's, Euclid Avenue screaming, one way downtown, one way the suburbs—my spirit sweating to escape and Fydor Karamozov murdered just as my customer arrives, all muscle and mirror sunglasses: "I want the Ford in back." My father told me stories about criminals on the lam who would need cars in a hurry. He didn't mind: "they always pay up front, cash." As usual, this junker needs a charge-up: the man twitches, Jesse wheels the gigantic battery charger over, cracks the hood, tightens the wires—it juices right up, and I feel the damp of hundreds and fifties. The customer peels out like a drag racer.

My first sale! This long-haired distracted son my father calls: *the last of the hippies* is worthy, and the old man will be proud; he is, he pats me on the back, offers me a cigar, claims in a puff of smoke I'll inherit the business yet, demonstrates the most important sales tactic: "if a customer looks at a car, don't approach immediately. If he bickers with the price, look him in the eyes and walk away, just walk away," straightening himself by way of demonstration as my customer returns, streaming as the hot sidewalks, blood-faced, pounding his fist on the desk, demanding back his money—he turned the engine off and it won't restart.

My father doesn't look up, cocksure: "Sorry sir, we sell our cars as is." I bury my nose deep into the ravings of Ivan Karamazov to the Grand Inquisitor. "This box here," my father mutters, staring at the form a second too long. "Well, I see it isn't checked." He points at me: "He sold you the car didn't he? Well, look at him." Both glare as they would a disobedient dog. "He doesn't know nothing."

Later, at home over dinner, my father snips sharply: "How can you be such a *meshuggener?*" What do you want to *be*, anyway?"

"A writer and a teacher," I blurt out.

"I'm glad," he fires back, biting down on his steak as if it was the word and not the piece of meat he was ferociously chewing, "you didn't say: *poet.*"

## 4. A Cast of Thousands

My dad's kid brother, Hy,
worked fourteen-hour days
at Cotton Club Soda Factory
through the Depression and the War,
dreaming of stardom. Eighteen,

wavy black hair, six foot six, dimples,
everyone's head would turn
when he'd stride like an undiscovered star
through the double doors
of Cork and Lenny's Delicatessen

where you would take a number
and order the smoked fish, the lox,
the spicy corned beef, the herring
in wine sauce and sour cream
from the old women in red *shmattes*

speckled with vanilla splotches,
faces patched with rouge and lipstick—
wishing all the customers a *mazel tov*
and filling the air with their *kibitz* song—
*You vant I should slice the challah?*

*What's the matter, here you think
it's not fresh?*—in the clatter
and clutter from the meat counter
and the *kvetching* in the corner booth
where the *alter kockers* gathered

and *kibutzed* about the *machers* and the *k'nockers*.
My father had his own parable

about the man who was paid a ruble
per day to wait by the Eastern Wall
for the Messiah: *"How can you work*

*for such low wages?" they asked the guy.*
*He replied: "Low wages, sure.*
*But at least the work is steady."*
His brother, though, hitchhiked all the way
for a role in *The Ten Commandments.*

He played a slave,
then went into real estate. Each year
it appears around Passover, like Elijah,
and we'd watch close,
my father suddenly pointing to the set:

*There he is!*
*No, wait, there he is!*
*No, no, I'm sure this time! It's him!*
all of us straining for the familiar face.
He's still the one everybody asks about.

Some days, when it's dark early,
my father comes home from the used car lot,
kicks the snow off, tells us how none would start
and it seemed his blood would stop
and we should all be in California.


*5. Instructions on Climbing Your Father's Garage*

At first sign of dark,
climb onto the window ledge—
flatten your hands

on the roof's peeled tar:
all of your body is muscle,
sweat and strain, until
you rise against this
downward stress. Stand
full length and walk
on the strange surface
twelve feet up, look down
through the basketball net
to the other side. See,
just a few feet beyond,
your father has switched on
the kitchen light: he paces
in and out of your vision,
looking for something, for you.
Turn to the far corner, face
the neighbor's back yard,
sit down, legs dangling
over the edge. Looking into
the millions of stars, count,
until he calls, your blessings.


*6. Coda: My Father Calls My Name in the Voice of a Bird*

A bird I can't identify
cries from the next field
its two notes: *Phil-up,*

*Phil-up,* the way my father
would caterwaul my name
up the stairs for supper.

I still hear him, though
from the other world,
clamor for me to gather

in the feasting. If so,
it would be Sunday night
and steak medium rare,

sautéed with onions,
fried potatoes on the side.
It was his meal

and as far of heaven
as in his life he'd believe.
He taught us to suck the meat

clean of the bone.
But what if these echoes
have nothing to do

with my father and me?
What if the bird is exclaiming
its own hunger from the spruce

and, as is most likely, sounds
like a familiar voice only because
I want, like everyone,

for my beloved dead to live again?

# THE *SHVITZ*

*for Mrs. Osburn's Zone and Traffic Marker Service*

If the Torah is our lives,
our portion was sung in that sanctuary
of a steam house by a *minyan* of ten
thirteen-year-old boys and a counselor,
a secular rabbi who knew the streets
like an emissary from the world
where our lives are already sealed.

He led us past the sign that still reads:
*Members Only*, listed in the phone book
as *The Russian Bath and Tea Room,*
but known to the initiates as *sweat*
in Yiddish, on 116th and Luke, our parents'
old neighborhood when all the world
was kosher and on Sabbath mornings

they walked in tennis shoes under
laundry drying above the street,
past houses of uneven boards
and sunken roofs, the fishmarket,
the famous Zeiger's Delicatessen,
before it changed, all except this small
brownstone, with a *mezuzah* on the door.

In back of the lockers I imitated his motions
as he took off his suit coat, muscles bulging
behind white shirt and tie, his pants,
the undershirt, the underwear, and I was afraid
to go on, to show myself in front of strangers.

*Come on,* he said, *here we're all the same,*
*underneath.* Once, late at night,

just we two gave each other backrubs
on his living room floor. My shoulder blades
felt like wings beneath his moist palms
as he rubbed down my back and around
the inside of my arms, kneading
my flushed skin with his fingertips.
I was one body touched by another body.

Here, cots with clean sheets lined
the central room. He instructed: after
we sweat, we rest. Adjacent, the dining area:
kosher pickles and hot peppers in bowls
under a photograph of the Wailing Wall:
after we rest, we eat. Steaks with garlic
broiled in the stove: Then we go sweat some more.

We were with history.
But all we knew was that we were naked
among men who were reading newspapers
or talking about how it was all changing
and the law was in our own hands.
Our counselor led us into the steam room
where old men sat on towels beside buckets

of cold water they'd pour over their heads
and fill up again. We began at the lower
bench, facing the hole in the wall where
the sandstones glowed like burning bushes,
then moved up, rising with the heat, daring
the others to lie full length at the top,
long as they could stand it, longer,

until the room was so full of gray mist
we became outlines of figures floating
in a secluded heaven, simmering out
all of our small tensions, and still he'd say:
*Throw in more water. It's not hot enough—*
our heads down, my hands, like his, gripping
splintered wood against the oncoming rush.

# ELOQUENCE

"... for I am slow of speech, and of a slow tongue."

—Moses to God

Born defective, roof of mouth
too splintered, a cracked
bowl, pallet cleft like
tabernacles and so my speech
is impeded, my S's slurred,
my R's never rounded out,
and I knew to repeat myself
like a foreigner, as if my first
was my second language.
Kids made their usual fun: *Listen*
*to the one with the bone*
*in his mouth.* In speech class,
I resisted reshaping the figures
my tongue made in the shelled
spaces of the cheeks, the air
between teeth, quivering upward
like a needle in its compass,
into the deep gulf of the North,
where I exiled unsaid syllables,
at home in their deformed privacy,
the way, I learned, the tongue of Moses
clung to its dome. Pharaoh
gave him a choice of gold or live coals.
No god, Moses reached for the coins,
but the angel descended to push
and fold his fingers over what
was torn out of the earth
and on fire, charring the flesh Moses
quickly pressed to his lips,

scorching his tongue, a small bush
burning. His brother was his voice,
his mouthpiece before the people,
but when he conversed with the silence,
as I write on this page, he wandered
off by himself and spoke alone.

*I was a Bilfield*, my mother begins,
starting with the name her father
gave her, *before I was a Terman.*

She is sitting at the kitchen table,
facing the clock with the Hebrew letters,
its poorly tuned motor a perpetual moan

in the background when the house
is full, louder when she's alone
among furniture and portraits.

*The names of Jews,* she says, *were for
their occupation, what they did.
A "feld" meant a large field. My grandparents*

*worked in a large field, green,
wildflowers, in summer. Austria-
Hungary. The* shtetl *I'm not sure of.*

*I have it written down somewhere.*
What happened to that name: Bilfield,
field? My mother keeps it tucked

between other names. Whenever
I do anything right—get up early,
set the table before she comes home—

I'm a Bilfield, a field with yellow
and blue and white, a meadow
in a country no longer there,

divided and portioned out like
its people scattered under the grass
or in other lands, their names diminished,

their language attenuating to hushes,
breaths stuttered into the ears
of children—phrases from a Yiddish

they strain to hear, like the story she tells now
about her grandparents Shmu-el
and Malka. Their portraits hang on the wall:

Shmu-el: gray streaks in a beard
that bunches past his white collar,
the black coat of the peasant

and the black square hat
because wherever he was
he was in the House of God.

His eyes stare into the future
as if it were an obligation.
And the other, Malka, for whom

my mother was named:
Malka, Mildred—
the first letter of the most recent dead

passes on, the rest of the name
we fill in for ourselves—so what
is left of us is an initial, one capital

letter, a sound signifying human
to remind us that we are spelled out
of those who came before—

Malka, sad-faced, babushka
wrapped around thin hair, looped
across tired breasts, the forehead

wrinkled and around the eyes
marks of claws, pupils staring
in slightly different directions,

the right tilted upward signaling
worship, the left off to the side
signaling caution and there's something—

these figures, inside their original frames,
sketched in pencil and charcoal,
dusted with one-hundred-year-old light,

something, not in the noses or chins,
the mouths fixed as if the barest smile,
a grin would be an effort—but something

in my mother's voice: *Shmu-el*
*was an elder—I have it written down*
*somewhere—and the Germans*

*lined him up and they shot him*
*and Malka came across with a son*
*they discovered to be tubercular*

*so the officials at Ellis Island*
*wouldn't let him in. Imagine—*
*she left these portraits with a relative*

*and made the long journey back*
*so the son shouldn't make the trip alone,*
*coughing up blood, both disappearing*

*on the other side of the waters*
*in the country of hardship, but where—*
*we can only guess.* My mother's eyes

turn and lock into mine: *Yes—*
her head nods to the rhythm
of the clock moaning: *we can guess.*

Some days you have to turn off the news
and listen to the bird or truck
or the neighbor screaming out her life.
You have to close all the books and open
all the windows so that whatever swirls
inside can leave and whatever flutters
against the glass can enter. Some days
you have to unplug the phone and step
out to the porch and rock all afternoon
and allow the sun to tell you what to do.
The whole day has to lie ahead of you
like railroad tracks that drift off into gravel.
Some days you have to walk down the wooden
staircase through the evening fog to the river,
where the peach roses are closing,
sit on the grassy bank and wait for the two geese.

# FOR GANYA

Hebrew for garden. The wise say to take another name
and hide it from everyone so that God can call us
in the night. You chose yours out of your calling,
Scrubgrass Road, Venango County, Pennsylvania,
across from the Amity Church and its cemetery,
where the road rises and gives the land its southern slope,
so what grows will be first to bud and last to frost.

Out of your life study, your real work, your daily art,
waking and sleeping, your thoughts and blood attending
to each season, rising in the first light, resting with the dark,
daylight animal, dream animal. Off Old Route 8,
between Clintonville and Mercer, Grove City and Franklin,
what the rural postal carrier calls *The Lord's Protected*.
Under the same slate commissioned to roof

this red brick one-room schoolhouse, *1884* carved
above the entrance, dating our dwelling the way
the *mezuzah,* slightly tilted, nailed to the maple doorpost,
is a reminder to teach words scripted from time's
other side and to speak of them and to bind them
as a sign and to wear them as frontlets
on the forehead the way birds are distinctively marked,

like these winter survivors lighting around the birdfeeder:
the fluffed up blue jay perched on the twisted blueberry bush,
the cardinal's occasional flame-flash, the surprise feather-
whistle of the mourning dove, its sleek neck jerking
at groundseeds, the woodpecker davening on the sycamore,
the omnipresence of the chickadees, the common juncos,
the snowbird hovering where wheatfield edges into wood

in the winged pages of a bedside book. From stiff leaves,
spruce cones, lopsided apples, hardened with the season.
From dried-out sunflower seeds whose stalks
only months ago were taller than our heads, taller
than the telephone wires, leaves large as tabletops,
from popcorn husks clothes-pinned to the greenhouse rope,
from canning and preserving, from consuming the past

in the present, from mint we transplanted from beside my Russian
grandmother's rented wrap-around porch: you took this name.
From eggshells and coffee grounds and carrot bits
in the compost pit we built with scrap lumber and fence wire.
From skunk cabbages that conceal their flowers in marshes
along the spring that feeds the pond where you showed me
the tadpoles as they one by one broke out of their sacs

and announced themselves to the water: *Ganya.*
From moody breezes, the meaningful weather, the invisible
spirits of the deer who in half-light leave their signatures
and night-huddle in clearings. From raccoon-in-the-corn fear,
rabbit fear, chemical-spray-from-neighbors fear. From fresh oak floors
and old oak burning off bone chill, its ash we scatter
on the garden snow. From everything becoming everything else.

From our previous lives, our deep griefs, our broken
hearts. From our renewed desires, our fierce attractions,
our mating calls and embarrassments, here we are,
magazines piling up in the corner, skullcaps and candles
stored in the cupboard, our property of good silences,
our casual arrangements, our serious talk, in the washed air,
in the fog hovering like a friendly animal among the arborvitaes.

From our privacy where we move by touch, allowing
the inner reaches, the bumps and bruises, the curves.

Before the day with its duties, the bells, the talk, the shuffling,
the visible sores. You are sinewy like ironwood, hard bark,
taut, tightened, stretched thin as the flesh over your cheekbones
my fingertips shape in the natural light. Your face is luminescent,
a flame illuminating its candle, water shimmering under close stars.

Before the gray light and the dust swirls, the scraping of bowls,
the spills, doors closing, the coughs and the news of bombs,
I massage your inner thighs, my tongue circling your small hairs.
Before the alarm, before the cold porcelain, the traffic
and the necessary anxieties, you open up your body and I enter.
Once, a robin beat on the window, saying there was vastness here.
Wings against glass said we could offer it further flight.

Once, another chirped in the chimney, chiding,
joining our conversation. But it was fear speaking,
out of the spine of the house. You opened the ash door:
orange-reddish breast and throat, streaked with black,
olive eyes spotted as the course grass and reeds and mud
it nests in. You grabbed hold of its feathers, its pulsing belly
against your pulsing palms, flung it back into its distance.

The dead students know we keep the schoolhouse unlocked.
They gather here as if still assigned. They recall days
when it was one great room to reassure themselves
that the Angel of Knowledge, for whom these bricks
were fired a half-mile away, carted in wheelbarrows,
stacked and mortared and pointed to last
centuries, the labor of learning, still Latinizes here.

The story goes that the builder Robert Sterret called it:
*Victory Two* because his wife wanted it someplace else:
the second time he ever got his way with her.
Leonard Riddle, the student badboy, told us this,

in his middle-of-the-pasture trailer the other side of Mill Road.
He chewed so much tobacco he had permanent lines
of dried-up juice stained on either side of his chin.

Cold mornings, he said, the teacher lit
the pot-bellied stove but some of the boys
arrived earlier, stuffed corn stalks down the chimney
for a day off. Said sixty years ago there weren't many trees.
You'd be five miles away and, after a day of wood gathering,
splitting, hauling, stacking, you'd gaze over the acres
at the schoolhouse and the church: always in view,

learning and God and knowing-what's-ahead,
like spring's arrival, each year, as recorded in the first book.
The genesis of coltsfoot, daffodils, the irises,
and the columbines. The struggle for the rare flower,
the trillium, secret all year but for its subtle passage.
Shaped in threes: leaflets, sepals, petals of its solitary star,
red or white, its only knowledge the knowledge of early spring.

We strained our eyes for it, brief rumor.
We risked our lives in the crevices, balancing ledges.
We examined the earth with our countless leanings,
among boulder and spring, slag chips and hidden lovers.
It wasn't until we gave up that it was revealed, in the marsh.
We lay in the damp and floated in its lily-herbs.
We licked hidden places, lolling in swampy love.

You said the garden is earned one spadeful at a time:
onions, thin as hairpins, germinating in flats and cellpacks,
barely visible under the grow lights: pumpkin rouge,
butternut squash, cucumbers, melon, lettuces, cabbage,
too-numerous-to-list tomatoes, peppers from pimiento to jalapeno,
cauliflower and broccoli and oregano and basil, and not to forget
the flowers: statice and asters and zinnias and nicotianas:

the every morning watering and soil inspections,
the farewell to the frost, the rototilling, the spreading
of horse manure, stringing rows and staking, hoeing
and weeding, the tucking-in with last year's straw.
*It's time to plant,* you said, holding the rocky dirt in your hand,
*when it sifts through your fingers. When it unshapes itself.*
The way I unshape myself

on this haybale. My study is a wheatfield. These words
are birdsong. Dawn is the title of this book, leaves
rustling near an open window. I record as it passes
the spring. Spider webs quivering in the apple tree.
Redwing blackbirds and robins and wrens architecting
their hidden palaces. I make certain commitments
about my future. I dwell on a song as it sparrows to the beanfield

and back again to its branch. My loved ones are twigs
and straw and deer hair I clasp in my mouth
to weave the nest that surrounds my dying. Ganya.
We are bulbs of light     say these yellow onions
we are wet with dew     say the early rose buds.
Says the mourning dove's flight out of the spruce tree.
In our beings we are brilliant.

Look up and examine the woman in the garden.
Her hands are soil in a raised bed. Consider the corridor
of light, the squirrel's scuttle on the beech tree,
teaching us to love our ties to their latest splendor.
Consider the hummingbird, who demonstrates how to tread
the air, the way he flickers, not as the buzzard
who swirls slowly over the roadkill, or even as the butterfly

in constant flutter like a flower petal wind-tossed,
but among these hollyhocks and sweet Williams, pausing
and posing, silent, staring into my face as if to suggest:

*You are not yet a flower. You cannot fill me with delight.*
We allow time to whiten us, to make us familiar
as this now summer grass, the turning constellations.
Beyond the fiftieth gate of reason, the quietudes,

the seventy faces of the Word, we stare into the miraculous,
our mouths slightly open, our eyes wet. Like Moses
through parted waters, we float across the air to our appointed tasks,
saints in our synagogue, chanting ancestral words.
As now, Sabbath dusk, a thin orange line seeps the horizon,
the crescent moon cradles its emptiness. Coffee.
Silence. The church across Scrubgrass gathers worshippers.

We sit on the porch swing and listen to the hymns, drifting
through a day of fluid time. Summer water. Sister and brother
toss the football, the older instructing the younger.
Their parents are singing jubilant for a life in heaven.
Beyond them, former congregants are already there,
their spirits marked by stones of various sizes and states of repair.
*That's it,* she says. *This way. See the spiral?*

They will play a long time before they enter the eastern door
of the white building and take their places in the pews and listen
to laughter much like their own through the open windows.
Now the garden flames a holy fire and the sky folds
its blue wings like a heron's in sleep. And even longer
before the western door opens and they settle in another life
beside their loved ones, who approach now, the service ended.

# SPEAKING TO BE HEARD

*for Etheridge Knight*

I

He was in the shower
and fifteen minutes late.
I could hear him drying off

and singing. My business
was to make sure he got there,
but I thought he'd think I was

just another white college
professor who didn't know
his work well enough.

An empty bottle on the dresser,
butts smashed into saucers.
Papers strewn on the mattress.

The stories: how he was strung out
and a thief and lived on the streets
of nowhere like Indianapolis.

How he had to visit the university
earlier than planned
so he could beat the cancer.

He stepped out, wrapped
in a towel—yes, I saw the leg,
scarred almost down to bone,

blue with clots and pus:
*Got it when a car hit me.*
*Dragged me clear ten feet.*


2


He is spotlit,
amplifying what he says
about the oral tradition,

voice like slivers
between the rails and crossties
after a train glides past:

poets speaking to be heard,
different from a page lying
flat in silence, but the spoken

is song, voice to ear, is history.
The voice is jail cell and splash
of light on the floor, is dope

and fucked up. It's balls
and snatch, brick and blood,
cracking with smoke and drink.

It's croak and spit and smooth
slide and cry in the words
it croons about its daughter.

3

I was in the joint once. Not
as him, but doing time
in my own way, teaching

composition for rent money.
Summer drought, sweat
staining like a second skin,

dust swirling across the yard.
Class was one level below
the gym where chests spurted

grunts and heaves, quick breaths,
animal strains, pounding,
groans from the stress.

No office hours. Each was awarded
two days off their sentence
for perfect attendance.

Walls were cracked like veins,
cigarette butts stomped out
into small black splotches.

They wrote about their trials,
some developing how they were wronged,
others the details of their penance,

and the way the curves,
undersides of their ladies'
thighs, would give way, at 3 a.m.,

alone in their cells, stroking
their own small hairs. One
looked me in the eyes and said:

*I killed someone.*
*You teach me good*
*because I'm going to write me a book.*

4

During a break, a few of them
were gathered in a circle
around a baby starling who'd dropped

from behind a drainpipe, a small
pool of oil on the pavement,
its black tissues shuddering,

wing bones snapped. Back inside,
in their mandatory blue shirts,
they brainstormed freedom,

their words white chalk on blackboard:
*sky, woman, space*. And now
they tell me he's dead, no

surprise, considering the system.
This is close as I can get, Etheridge,
not enough, the other side of the bars.

Guards wait outside the door
of this room without acoustics,
where we read our private scratchings, aloud.

# FOR IRINA RATUSHINSKAYA

*I went in a healthy woman. But they took care of that.*
Citing one of her poems as evidence, seven years.

Spare lines about wearing the body's rags before god.
She is thinning down to muscle. Solitary

can't shut her up—she scrapes with her nails
verses into scraps of soap,

recites each poem like someone
who writes what she herself is afraid to read.

She rinses the bar clean and flushes it down
into the sewers. The authorities never search below the surface.

The poems pile up, so many she has to remember—
the titles, the order: ten, twenty-five, a hundred,

two-hundred and fifty, eyes fixed into a thick
wall, chanting over and over in her head a rosary of words,

swaying in the blank face of her own execution.
*It's not difficult. It's my calling.* They are smuggled out,

one by one, a whispering of alliteration and assonance,
smooth touch of vowels, soft sibilance from cellmate's lips

into cellmate's ear, heart by heart, the words passed
in memorized passage all the way into the other world.

## THIS SWEATER

Stretching into my new used white sweater
I purchased at an AIDS thrift shop
on Columbus Avenue in the West Seventies,

a slight coffee stain on the front,
a small hole on the bottom in the back,
lighter than a heavy coat,

heavier than a light coat,
perfect for this unexpected warmth
of early January, balmy as spring,

snug around the chest and arms,
I wonder who was the bulky man
with the fatal disease

warmed by this sheep's wool,
matching my measurements.
He wore it in but didn't wear it out,

then rejected it with everything else,
left to others, I hope to a lover,
to worry over and decide

not to keep, perhaps because
he couldn't stop touching its emptiness.
A donation rather, passing it on

to another, to me. Not unusual
to inherit the garment of the dead
or to wonder if I also will acquire

a small portion of the wearer's soul,
we who are so similar in size,
sharing as we do the same taste

in our apparel. And if whoever loved him
happens to witness me now, fully
embraced in its warmth, still holding

its shape, is reminded
of that soul? And if that memory
makes him suddenly live again?

# THE OLDEST BROTHER LESSON IN THE WORLD

*for Stuart Terman*

In the room without heat the desk's cherry wood
warmed his body all night until the pale skin of dawn

found his face pressed beside the book opened
to drawings of the skeleton he studied through

the noises of that house, the screams of our father
calling him down to dinner. Ten years younger,

upset with one crisis or another, I carved our name
in the surface but he said furniture is alive like us

if we allow it to breathe and pass it on
the way it was made. Near an open window he wore

the scratches away with steel wool, his fingers precise as if
treating bruises on skin, brushed on the stain

with delicate surgeon's eyes, the wet streaks shimmering
like roses in the sun. It was what he left me,

smudged with the invisible smoothings of his palms,
the imprint of his ghost-ear listening to the tree in the wood,

what I listen for now, sanding my own splinters
and chipped edges, the flaws he taught me how to re-touch.

Some say as brothers get older they get more distant,
meaning we grow out of our childhoods,

when we sat in the same waters
and he rubbed my tender flesh with soap.

This will last as long as memory lasts,
and now that it is here written down, longer,

and anyone who cares can imagine an older
brother cleaning the younger as has been done

according to custom throughout the centuries.
It will last as long as the oldest brother lesson in the world will last,

the story our mother taught us about the two sons
who wound up wandering apart in two separate worlds.

Her own two brothers stopped speaking over something
or other and the years hammered the nails of their refusal

harder into their wounds until one died and became
bones that spoke less than the silence of the flesh.

Does his body cry to his brother from the ground?
Is cursing a brother the same as cursing yourself?

Is looking into a brother's face like looking into water
and seeing your own death? Are brothers two wings

of a great bird? Does each carry inside of him the other
half of the secret of how to live a righteous life on earth?

*Do I look like anyone?* he asks,

as he swoops the long spoon into the peas,
lifts it a few inches
and holds it steady to pour
onto the tray of the next famished mouth,
shouts to George for more
as his supply empties down.

I'm the bread and donut man
in this assembly line of volunteers
who gather for our three hours
of weekly service and socialism:

Jose the finger-pointing Filipino
who pours the punch and repeats:
*The wages of sin is death*
and only reads *Paradise* from the *Comedy*,

*for his description of heaven,* he says, *and light*;

Jake the Buddhist, who scrapes the dishes
as they are returned, saves whatever
appears untouched for someone else's

insatiable hunger;
            Sal, who tells me he was on the other side
of the line, meaning he was one of the thousand
who form every morning single-file around this Church
of the Apostles, up 9th Avenue and around

28th Street,
      *like the snake,* he chants,
looking out the window beyond Crack Park,

*cursed above the beasts of the city*
*to eat dust all the days of its life.*

And their eyes are filled with dust,
      drugged and sleepy,
bodies stiff from sidewalk cardboard sofas.

The peaman, it turns out, looks like Albert Einstein,
the shaggy white hair and white mustache,
pronounced nose and dark sad eyes.

*I'm an actor*, he explains. *They pay me to look like the genius.*

He shows me his card: $E=mc2$
*Equity equals many characters,*

and I'm honored to be near even the resemblance of the man—
not because I understand relativity
and the contradicting theories of light,

but because of how steady he is with a spoon,
filling each helping to the brim,
as if each portion should be equal

and abundant.

I paused before The House of Sages,
beside the boarded-up synagogue,
on my walk down East Broadway

toward the river for relief
from the heat's tidal wave.
*Founded in 1922*, the slab stone says,

the year of my father's birth.
The white sign above the caged
door announces in Hebrew

the Polish *shtetl* of its origin.
Near the bolt lock and intercom
a spray of white paint:

swirls and loops like lopsided
hearts and question marks
and the street's fevered talk.

Through the cracked window
men in black were poring
dusty faces over pages spread

open like stilled wings,
quivering bodies revealed
in this late afternoon glare shafting

the Lower East Side. I wanted
to enter there, to assume
the white robe and crown, to bow

down low before the open Ark
and touch the book
with my scarf and place my fingers

to my lips and kiss there.
I wanted all of this, to arrive
and hear my name called,

son of my father, in the first
language and all the silence after.
I stood in the sidewalk's fire.

The gate opened. A bearded shadow
appeared and I stole inside
before it closed like a cloud behind me.

I peeked into the sanctuary
of the sacred and a sage
was reading a newspaper

the way my father or I
relaxed at table, long legs
stretched out on the dark oak,

feet crossed. Another
was solving a crossword puzzle,
inquiries in the holy tongue.

What questions down?
What questions across?
Were the answers printed

in the next life? A few
were bending their torsos
down and up, down and up,

as if lettering with their bodies
some unfathomable word
or testing out a new law of physics:

if you rub flesh with air, a spark.
Soon, first one then another
turned toward my direction,

all staring, eyes fixed, curious
at my intrusion. Should they touch
their foreheads to the eastern wall

or call the police? Briefly all the noise
of New York became one word
which filled the room, our only world.

*from* BOOK OF THE UNBROKEN DAYS

Like no other time of year,
we gather to remember
who we are and where we belonged,
migrating the way certain birds
will return to the same place

the same time each year.
Our sanctuary was so full
they had chairs off to the side,
facing a wall, the cantor's liturgy
amplified, booming across

the domed House of God the way
we imagined God's voice
would have bellowed down
from the mountain or out of a bush.
We took our cues from others—

they rose and we knew the great Book
was taken out of the ark and lifted
above the rabbi's shoulders—they sat
and we knew it was returned
and the silk curtains closed delicately.

Ten years old, I looked into the thick
black book, wondering at the lines
and dots, and why they all read
from right to left. My mother
moved her lips and turned the pages and so did I,

thinking only of how I missed
the World Series, again. My father
had his book closed, head down.
I whispered to my mother, hand
on stomach: *I feel sick.*

My father offered to take me home.
We squeezed between worshipers out
into the still warm October air, the dark,
the large spaces the streets offered.
What we talked about I don't remember.

Only how clear with stars the night was.
And how big and tall was that man
made out of meat and potatoes,
and how the whole way home we strolled
side by side into the New Year.

*

The woodpecker investigates
        the maple like a rabbi
a complicated passage.
        They have slipped out of time
into a place of their own longing,

examining their texts
        for the kernels, the sweet meat.
Their hunger is insatiable, like
        this wind, which will not
settle in one brilliant tree,

but pursues its desire
        ravishing the leaves completely.
Is that what we mean by worship,

our skins saturated
in each others' juices,

embracing until we are spectacular,
then flame's afterglow?

\*

A few leaves
hear their calling
and begin their next life.

The last water lily
blossoms, an old triumph,
the days another series

of hours that include us.
The sky has taken a step back.
We are in the wind now.

My child points
to the dust swirling
in the shaft of sunlight.

My child: body-of-laughter,
door-opening-into-my-answer,
witness-to-my death.

Alterations of clouds, wheels,
blue jays screeching
from the drooping sunflowers.

The season consumes us.
It presses and squeezes us dry,
like apples into cider.

Somewhere there's a mountain
for each of us, and a well,
somewhere we will move as air

flowing through the field's room,
water falling into greater water,
the silence as large as our longing.

                    *

The house without a clock,
the flourishing scarves,

the swaying shadows,
the book cupped in the hands,

the pages on fire,
the choir of the blessed.

I was a candle of constancy,
a flame against September's spectacle.

I was a short word
in the service,

awe in a child's body,
a small scroll lifted

into the silence
we rose up towards.

I stood in the sacred
perpetual, paused,

stared into our portion,
and sang.

# THE FAMOUS RUSSIAN-JEWISH WOMAN
# POET TERMANOVSKY

If you found out your great grandmother
was a poet, if there was one obscure book
you discovered one off-day at the bottom

of a dusty cardboard box, in the corner
basement room, covered up by pickle jars,
slid behind your father's war uniforms,

a volume slim as a small hand, the cover
a faded blue, layered and sealed with mold,
the pages tearing with a touch, the letters

in Yiddish, and there's her name: *Termanovsky,*
your name, before shortened by the authorities,
the way they'd slice off anything unpronounceable.

Termanovsky, the famous Russian-Jewish woman
poet, her daguerreotype on the title's facing page,
her face, the one you recognize from worn photos,

but younger, a beauty, no babushka—a frilled scarf
wrapped around the neck, her dark thick hair
flowing from beneath a tilted-to-one-side beret,

a few strands loose across her cheeks, dangling
from her lips a cigarette. She examines the strange
letters, lines, stanzas, wonders about

the pressure of her fingers pressing the pen
to the paper, between the poverty and the pogrom,
the praying for a relative to sponsor her over,

the baking of the bread she had to peddle
in the marketplace, having to worry about who
would print and publish poems by a woman

named Termanovsky about being a girl
in the *shtetl,* the smell of herring and challah
rising, horses and wagons in the open air,

the mud streets, the learned huddled toward
the eastern wall, old men in black coats, how
it shamed her to have to sit on her side

of the synagogue—even if she had the space,
even if she had the time to save her moments
in words, the way she kept buttons in a box,

and was assured of the support to write them all down.

And maybe that's why, after my grandfather
the junkman passed away, she contented herself
with my parents' basement: a small stove,

a refrigerator, an ironing board, an electric
heater, a sewing machine—a Singer,
foot-pedaled, like the ones in this photograph

where Jewish immigrant women of childbearing age
assembled after the stormwind of 1905 ripped them
from the *shtetl* where the Bible was daily news.

And in their wooden synagogues and homes, sunken
around the marketplace, the streets winding tortuous
as a Talmudic argument, the hard years would give way

to redemption. But all they knew was massacre
and forced conversion, so they departed, hungry
to earn a living, America on their mouths.

Here, in this enormous tenement of high temperatures
and bad lighting, gaslights hang from ceiling pipes,
blazing the black machines: workshop,

sweatshop, square room of concrete and brick,
the claustrophobic air absorbing their exile—
overcrowded and everywhere cloth, cloth, cloth,

spread out, shaped into garments, hung limply
on racks, seven dollars a week, in the dirt and dust,
fingers gathering and ruffling, basting and pleating,

embroidering, feet tapping in rhythm on iron grills, treadling
pedals, a seamstress dance, shoulders hunched over
into premature curvature of the spine, back-aching,

hair tied back in buns, hands spooling string,
a constant motion, joints itching their way to arthritis.
A million miles from birth, semi-skilled,

and there were always replacements.
And when would they look into a holy book?
Do they *kibitz* about their peddler boyfriends

as they risk tuberculosis, the tailor's disease?
Do they fear the soup kitchens?
Some look toward the camera, others persist

at their needling, unaware that eighty years later
one of their grandchildren will identify his own:
near the only window, wearing a *shmatte*

over a cotton dress. She will repair my clothes
from her supply of worn fabric or replace a button
from the tin box stored in her basement closet.

Ignoring the commotion, she will lean toward
her own steady center, lick and follow the thread
through the eye, the way she labored, dark

to dark, all her life, save for the Sabbath.

SINGER AMONG THE PIGEONS

There are laws against you,
how you shit over everything—
noisemakers, nuisances, stalkers

of rooftops and statues, stealing
underfoot, gathering in gangs,
subject to regulations, legal

poisons, experimental research.
But then: *Who knows?* he said,
your spokesman, your messiah—

*In the next generation, perhaps*
*we'll all return as hungry pigeons.*
Feeding you on the corner of Broadway

and West 86th on his daily walk
to the corner table at the café
where he met his characters

for a vegetarian lunch—potatoes
and knish, a glass of cold tea—
you perched in gutters, waiting.

He was reliable as the faded
bathrobe and shabby slippers
he wrote in, typing his stories

straight through, as dependable
as his destroyed streets of Bilgoray,
the houses with low roofs covered

with tiles and moss, the rooms
of his own house, the bookshelves,
all the holy books, each word and letter,

as faithful as the Yiddish scholars and peddlers,
the dialect he spoke to you in, the *shmeggege,*
convinced you'd understand him, the *putz,*

speaking in a dead tongue to rejected birds.
*God's creatures*, he called you, an odd bird
himself with his flappy ears and wide eyes,

pale cheeks and beaked nose, awkward,
like his heroes, a bit of *shlemiel*, like Gimpel,
ugly, like you, a *luftmensch* living on air,

his bald head, you all agreed, a good target.
Once, one of you landed on his hat: *a pigeon
wouldn't land on just anyone*, he asserted—

*They can distinguish a Jewish writer
and wouldn't do anything to hurt him.*
That's the way he thought, this believer.

Some of you might even be his ancestors,
his grandparents the rabbis or his mother—
though it was forbidden—the Talmudic scholar,

his father the wise man of Korchmalna Street.
Some of you may even have been all the Jews
he left behind, the ones he couldn't save,

and now, perhaps one of you—which one,
among the tens of thousands scattered
and hungry throughout the city?—

coos in a language so stubborn it will not die.

Tonight after an all-day rain the world
seems far off and even my dead father
has retired back to the pinochle game
he plays with his older brother Nate
and that policeman Zuresky and Aunt
Florence's Uncle Joe, who even alive
was always unemployed but wore
the same brown suit and porkpie hat
and always had a stack of *Playboys*
stashed on the floor of the back seat
of his Plymouth. When I glanced at one
he warned that it was a bad habit:
*It gets you excited*, he said, *and that
costs money.* He'd always visit,
widowed or divorced I never knew,
talking about the track. I was too young
to inquire any further, his body thin
as a shadow, face pale, soft-spoken
and serious, smoking and playing cards
with Uncle Nate and that policeman Zuresky
and my father, who turns back now
from all my inquires and tells Uncle Joe
to stop shuffling and deal.

My mother is forgetting herself,
at first little by little, then large pieces
of her life disappearing, emptying out
like those black raspberries we picked

on the edge of the woods. We raced
the crows, avoiding the grapevines
and thorns, straining our fingers, eating
half our harvest on the way home.

Soon she will forget my face and voice
and that will be all—I will be as gone
from her life as before her first thoughts
of the future. Once, a killdeer

distracted us from its young, black
rings around its neck, white belly,
black eyes ringed with orange. It lay
on its back and folded one white

wing and pretended it was wounded.
*Go back to your own lives*, it said.
*There's still time to know how a rose
unfolds its mystery or to practice*

*reading a spider's web*. Still time.
Remember loss as distant as wherever
the voices on the radio came from?
I'd listen, my head against the play-

by-play, my mother cleaning dishes
in the sink, listening to her Jerry Vale . . .
If we didn't love so fiercely,
we'd be as accepting as the grass

soaking the rain from an hour ago,
as the volunteer gladiola flaming
against the doorframe, as the streaked
hummingbird supported only by air.

Winter afternoons in front of the heater,
my small body settled into her body,
the windows frosted, the living room
dimly lit. Fierce love, how it defeats us.

All the sages advise against it.
They lived in continual ecstasy,
laboring in the eternal, scribbling
volumes about the face and beard

of God. The world was not enough,
their names and their loved ones' names
ground down with their bones
into the soil. But in their toil, what pleasure!

They knew awe and the celestial throne,
the heft and height and weight
and shoe size of the Holy of Holies,
how wide His face, how long His hair.

We'd fall asleep on her large bed,
streaks of light sifting through the shade.
Tremble, and be as the rain-soaked grass,
as the sweet Williams, as the apple tree's

shadow lengthening, as the sun sliding
beyond the slate roof—my mother
is forgetting herself, first little by little,
then large pieces of her life disappearing—

she tells me: *In my nurse's uniform*
*I walked arm-in-arm with my brother*
*in his navy-whites, saluting neighbors,*
*past the old shul, to the drugstore . . .*

*we sat near the open window*
*and I ate all the ice-cream I wanted . . .*
her face flushing, as if the chocolate
on her tongue was dissolving into rapture.

There it is now, catching the first of the dark.

Frost and relentless rains, wedged between two branches
after the hard fruit has been picked or fallen
and the great exodus of the leaves,

allowing the wind to work its way
through straw, deer hair, mud, twigs, grass,
and the silence.

      No longer functional,
it serves a greater uselessness—
bowl of air, cup of snow.

All spring long its builder swooped
orange breast from woods to nest to woods.

Now a stranger is perched
on its edge—wren or nuthatch, too dusky
to be distinguished, brief stay, quick flight.

Constructed in light, surrounded by white blossoms,
it protected, while the weather favored, its singing soul.

Now what does a house do without its bird?

The child we journeyed
half-way across the world
to raise as our own now
offers us the first flower

of the season. She holds it
tightly in her hand,
a small piece of her new earth:
coltsfoot, wild and yellow,

like the mustard flowers
they cultivate in the land
of her birth where peasants
irrigate the watery fields

in blue coats and straw hats,
some with babies strapped
with simple cloth on their backs,
not like the way I carried her

in my framed backpack
into a small village
of a few mud huts, each bare
except for large bags of rice

and old men sitting on the floor
around a mahjong board
and a candle, perhaps a house
like the one where she was born,

each having the same quality
of natural light, shoes placed
neatly outside the entrance.
This is the life she won't live,

laundry drying above the square,
hay stacked neatly, a water buffalo
roped to a tree, mud-caked
from the nearby paddies and, beyond,

the skyscrapers of the city,
some with cranes on their roofs
to construct more and more stories.
We snapped as many photographs

as we could to show her at least
a few slices of her lost world.
Maybe it was wrong of us to try
to capture anything at all of what

would make her long for more
because we can never return her
to the source of her beginnings,
the blood and bones of her origin,

except with whatever we tell her
that will make up the story of her life:
how two ancient men with crinkled faces
came out of their huts to pose with us

in front of the obliging water buffalo,
framed by the afternoon mustard flowers
that spread out into the architecture
of the immediate distance.

# MY RUSSIAN-JEWISH GRANDPARENTS AND THE BIRTH PARENTS OF OUR CHINESE CHILD MEET AT A CAFÉ AND DISCUSS OUR CHILD'S FUTURE

Schmu-el and Malka and our child's
Chinese birth parents are sipping tea
at a café somewhere between the Pale
Settlement of Russia and central-rural China.

They speak in signs and gestures, swirling
arms like dancers, shaping fingers into figures,
standing up and swaying, contorting bodies
to emphasize some obscure point, even

employing pauses and long silences to further
the conversation. The men gesture:
my grandfather's *yarmulke* is as black
as I imagine our child's birth father's hair.

The women continue to fill their husband's cups
and stare off into the distance.
The men agree on the major issue:
each will have to sacrifice their darlings,

their children—send them away, across
miles of land and ocean, into a realm further
and more unfamiliar than they could understand
even in their own tongue, a place perhaps

like those faraway and never-never lands
in the stories of each of their childhoods:
palace on a cloud, temple beyond the stars,
Jerusalem or Shangri-la. It's better

to think of that strange country this way
than to ponder the potential dangers—
strangers in strange lands, years of forced labor,
the poverty and destitution they themselves

know something about, each in their own way,
these farmers and peddlers, each of them know
dark to dark. Their gestures are more subtle
and sophisticated now, they even forget

and sometimes break out into their Yiddish
and Mandarin, which sounds as exotic
as a gathering of multicolored birds
singing through the tea's steam.

The bill, which is grief, arrives.
They agree to split it.
They accompany each other to the gate
that opens out into their separate centuries.

Through unfathomable signs, they gesture to meet again.

# FIRST DAY OF SPRING AND THE SECOND GULF WAR

As the birds were singing
the bombs were dropping.

You could hear birds singing
before and after the bombs

dropping, not during. You
could hear the bombs dropping

in-between the singing birds,
and you knew the bombs

were dropping and the birds
were singing at the same time

but you couldn't hear them both
at once. They told you what

kinds of bombs were dropping
but they didn't tell you what

kinds of birds were singing.
It was dawn in the ancient land

and then there were birds
and then there were bombs

and then there were birds again.

# ALTERNATIVE TEN COMMANDMENTS

Thou shalt walk with your love on summer evenings before supper
      to the pond with the many peepers.

Thou shalt sit in silence and listen to deep-throated trills chorusing
      their frog spirits from homes of leaves and sticks and water.

Thou shalt observe the gradual emergence of the Big Dipper, star by star.

Thou shalt not long for anywhere else.

Though shalt clear the mind of affairs of business and duties.

Thou shalt look from the ground to your lover's face, and press your lips there,
      and your tongue, and open your face to your lover's lips and tongue.

Thou shalt not be afraid of flashing lights of deer spotters and broken pickups.

Thou shalt slowly rise and, bopping to the frog's song, shimmy to the pond
      until the wheat field swallows your shadow.

Thou shalt fulfill the frog's longing and make your bodies bare, and slide
      into the water and glisten.

Thou shalt remain until your heartbeats slow down, and the moon appears
      above the surface.

# SOLSTICE

*for the Barkeyville Triangle*

Because we are moving through the waters of our lives.
Because of neighbors around a fire, a drum in each lap.
Because this is the brightest dusk we have known all year,
we tap our congas and kilambas, we clap, clatter, and racket,
we beat a ruffle and establish our rhythm, slapping the steerhide,
a pulsing pow-wow purging our accumulated pressures,
the djembe and the akaiko and the rumdrum and the rattles.
And some clicked sticks and some made whistles and flutes
with their hands and someone blew the didgeridoo. Because
we are alive we make music, we announce our joyful uproar
that is all-at-once the history and hieroglyphics of our hearts.
Because each of us holds down a day job. We've replaced
slate tiles and nailed in two-by-fours and counseled souls
who thought they were lost, pounded in tomato stakes and
spoken calmly to a weeping child, handled a backhoe
until baptized in our own waters. We've worked hard
for our wages, run our errands, dusted or considered dusting,
and each of us has at some time or another felt the lingering
of the light, each of us have measured our tempos with the pulses
of this longest day of the year. Because the winter, as expected,
lasted longer than our expectations. Because the spring was way too wet
and the frost moved in to live with us and nobody got the seeds in on time.
Because we are also the force that will not stop accumulating,
this insistence toward our own fulfillment. What is this that keeps us
building more rooms? Planting more seeds? Raising more children?
What is this that keeps us turning over our earth? We know
we are dying. Some of us are breaking down right now. Some of us
have had limbs removed and the cancer has shot up our spines,
this hour some of us are watching our own hearts turned inside out
and squeezed dry. We know the chaotic smugness of the dark apartments.

We know the way the shattered edges of a lightbulb feel in our palms at
    3 a.m.
We know how words can lay splattered like vomit on our own clothing.
There is no accounting for how all this gets layered in with the way
we watched the full moon appear piece by piece until it was fully realized.
Like when you stare at a face the contours of the bones clarify.
Because we know we have somehow made it to this moment
though we don't know how, or why. Because we all have our theories.
Each of us will sit you down and look you in the eyes and explain
for hours what is really an elaborate summary of how we came to be alive
at this particular place and time. Because the lettuce picked an hour ago
has gone to our heads, what with all that sunlight and soil digesting
through our systems, all that leafy succulence breaking down
and changing us. Because the sky has become the color of the fire.

Because we do not believe in original sin,
we'll praise these sweltering afternoons
picking blueberries with our daughter.

She picks all she can reach, having learned
to distinguish the blue from the green,
pebbles the sky washed in her hands,

the corn stirring in its tassels, the birds
whistling their arias, her new teeth sinking
into soft skins. How did she learn to want

such sweetness? Two nights in a row
she flew out of her crib, or did she tumble
onto the floor because she leaned her body

forward out of so much yearning?
The piercing scream didn't say. All we knew
was there she was, out of her cage.

When she sees a plane or a bird she points
and stares upward as if calling our attention
to whatever is soaring, the way she suddenly

directs us to the hummingbird in the hollyhocks
as they open out one atop the other, black wings
ascending a ladder of purple-pink blossoms

taller than we are, their stiff stalks stretching
straight out into the stars. Now my wife sings
our daughter to sleep, chimes sprinkling

like a celestial composition at the wind's
decree. I don't know how else to be grateful
for this life other than to compare it

to something fantastical, like being perched
on a swallow's wing or slipping underwater
on a bluegill's back or dispersing like pieces

of cloud or huddling in an oat grain
throughout the life of an August afternoon,
unfolding into something impossible,

the season's end—a chill, the first goldenrod
and ironweed, the crickets insisting, forcing us
into conclusions. Time snaps a tablecloth

out from under the dishes, the silverware
and wine glasses, the two lit white candles—
they stay their place, trembling. A buzzard

circles the cornfield, talons outspread, grim reaper
in a mid-summer Sunday morning, floating
through the watery air in smooth strokes,

attentive to the silence and the choir harmonizing
about their savior in the church across the road.
It's enough to watch the ripples the tadpoles make

as they skitter toward their invisible canyons.
We want to turn our backs to the leaves
parachuting like large seeds and the road

where the school bus slows down its inevitable
yellow myth. Summer unbroken like water,
like the sky before a vapor trail,

like deep sleep, summer like love that happens
or the way the gathering dusk gives way
to the first stars, the way the frog is immersed

in what sustains it, or how the earth feeds us
with its thorny bushes of black raspberries.
We change our light clothes for heavy pants

and sweatshirts, under the enormous sun, picking
and scratching for the taste of sweet tongues,
filling a pail, choosing the ones the color

of nothing, black flowers, tiny clusters like fish eggs,
the shape of pepper grains, pearls of night,
taking them home to mash and bake and slice

and top with vanilla ice cream—this is entering
the narrow door saying summer has not been wasted.
Summer is one long novel, thick with many plots—

turkey feathers and a nest of mourning doves
still trapped in their shells, fallen into the grasses,
the spider's drama in the corner of the porch.

Follow a row of tasseled corn into its point
of vanishing, follow a child into her life.
What keeps us from being overwhelmed

by how loss streaks through our dailiness?
Farmer Felix on his tractor, steadying the cutter,
plowing like a small ship, Neighbor Joshua cultivating

his beans after the long shift on the day job,
Mildred Dewalt in her purple hat and square sunglasses,
puttering down the dirt road in her golf cart to gossip,

retired Mr. Riddle planting his sweet corn—there he is,
pulling out with his bare hands all that damned quackgrass,
Umberto salvaging his twelve hours a day on his stone sculpture,

Rick Steigerwald hauling up a beam for his boy's play set—
he will measure it exactly, eyes squinted and focused,
he will not be defeated, not one of them will be stricken down.

So: at the beginning of this enormous century
we're eating vegetables we picked an hour ago.
This is the moment of celebration and the victory

over the nothingness we could have been
and will be, in this house removed from the road, home
to dragonflies and sparrows, two weeping willows

and a hundred and fifty spruce, where we begin
our future life, a little less panicked, and though
we are inadequate to the day, mostly distracted,

caught up as we are in the inscrutable snapdragons—
the yellow ones, brilliant as sunrise, color
of finches in flight, unobtrusive as finches

concealed in the upper stories of the pines—
I am presumptuous enough to describe
my wife washing our child in the cold creek,

under hemlocks, north of our everyday duties,
their two bodies giving shape to the dark.
I gathered wood, watching the sparks catch,

listening to the squeals and the nonsense.
I wanted this summer to be unbroken.
I wanted to settle the question once and for all.

I wanted the angel with the broken hip
to descend and challenge me and I wanted
my name to change to some purer sound

that would signify this happiness, that would mark
each cricket singing in its invisible chamber,
each flake of ash accumulating in that stone circle.

If I could save something small, something
insignificant and keep it a secret, something
to return to when our lives become strange to us,

something like the way the nicotianas at night
float their sweetness through our open windows.
Or simply a single pair of our child's blue jeans,

size two, spread out and pinned to the clothesline,
one end hooked to the house, the other end
looped around a branch of the backyard apple tree.

One child's pair of blue jeans framed
against the absolute blue of the sky—
and that's it, if we can take that into the next life . . .

An old woman wearing a garden hat is digging
out chicory, prolific on the roadside,
shaped like stars, blue as dragonfly wings.

She's placing it in a five-gallon bucket
as the afternoon for this one instant stops its course.
Soon goldenrod will rear their tips,

but for now the world vibrates
on its amber oat field, absorbing the shadows
of arborvitae and the swallowtail exhibits

its exotica on the air lighter than swallow down.
You look up and it is there.
So: this is what the hours have been spinning!

And we thought they were passive as cows
in the field, seen up-close, patient as good parents,
permanent as myth. Listen: a bird is telling you

its name and where it is among the trees.
Look up from your book about the perishing city
and step out to its slender call, the warm breeze

alerting you to its particular season, the ripples
describing their own agonies. Those pockets
of air into which the water lilies blossom foretell

their emptiness and how the dead are complete
in their ambitions. Once there was a place all the stories
lived. Someone whispered them. You went there.

One season collapsing
into another. Summer is giving itself
up, exhausted from its abundance.

These days are what we have left,
light softer than absence.

In this small book
you gave me when I had no other,

I will write until it is filled
with my desire

as I filled myself inside of you
mornings when our bodies broke into waves.

Before it passes, before our memories fail,
corn leaves browning back into soil,
sunflower heads drooping, before
the seasons of the slow heartbeats

and the shocks, before the years frail
like worn coats, and thin into patches,

let me say these words to you
after some exhausted day of hands and eyes,
after you have informed the rooms

with all that you know—

\*

Showering the podium
with spit and the hammers
of his fists,
the founding rabbi commands us—

in a rage that must have been Isaiah's—

into action. Enough
of debating, enough of questions
and contradictions, enough
of our lethargy.
Enough of our paralysis.

*For ye shall be as an oak fadeth*
*and as a garden that hath no water.*

\*

How can I write your gardens?

Your roses, daylilies, irises,
nicotianas, columbines, zinnias,
phlox, cosmos are too much

and I lose myself in this profusion,
the way the newborn calf
sucks violently on the nipple of the bottle
I try to steady in my shaking palms.

       *Rejected*
is what her mother did to her
when the other twin was born dead.

*They should've rubbed the live one,*
the farmer says, *all over*
*with the afterbirth,* meaning

the mother wouldn't walk away
from her own odor—flesh
of her flesh, fluid of her fluid—

back to the pasture to graze
and feed and lie down with the rest.

The ones that live remind us of loss.

*

*I can't feel my edges*, she says,
me inside her.
*You are my edges*, I reply.

*

The garden in late summer,
the moist straw we slide our fingers into
for the pulse of the red potato smothered
in soil, tomatoes flaring the red our skins flush
when our flesh announces: *consume me.*

The future can't swallow enough of our skins,
saying: *Tongue the juices now—one second more*

*and all of this perfection will collapse.*

*

*They worship the works*
*of their own hands,* the rabbi bellows:
*that which their fingers have made.*

*

We gather black raspberries,
sweet-of-the-fruit, juice-on-the-tongue
ripeness, pick-and-lick of our overflow,

the wet places of our wanting.

*

I walked out into the shadowed afternoon

and meditated on *sacred* and *hour* and *brittle*.
Down the gravel road I pondered: *accursed*.
Each syllable, as in *sacrifice*, compelled.

I said *landscape* and *severance* and *abandon*.
My companion would have offered *reverence*
so I sounded *splendor* and *fragile*.

*Absence* came out *altar*.
I looked up at the sky and shouted: *immensity*.
How did it translate later into *fractured* and *provisional*?

The crows cried out: *regret*.
Or was it *dispersion* and was it rather the grass?
I wondered: *dust*. The response: *ceaseless*.

*

Over the glory shall be a covering.

Under the white-bricked dome, thin membrane,
interior of an eggshell . . .

To look up into the synagogue ceiling,
shaped like a white skullcap,

steadied by stories of space,
and count each stone there one

by one is as enormous an effort
as wondering in early autumn
afternoon about the afterworld.

For both, you have to crane your neck
like an odd bird
and squint.

*

Not more than ten handsbreath tall,
according to the instructions
associated with our birth,

we construct our house of one room—

two-by-fours and cinder blocks,
one wall the side of a barn,
nails hammered in just enough
so a strong wind can tear it down.

Cornstalks, hollyhocks, blue spruce branches,
pine needles for the roof,
opening natural skylights for stars…

decorated with morning glories
and black-eyed Susans, secured
with blueberry bush netting.

Here we ingather,

take our meals, consider
everywhere is our home,

how thin the walls between inside
and outside, one world drifting
in and out of another.

*

Our bodies scarred and flushed,
drenched with lovesmell, we are heft and light,
limbs entangled like branches after a wind.

Where are we at the moment of arrival?
Are we where longing rests?
Does desire meet its demand?

I am on top of you,
or, the world spinning as it does,
you are on top of me.

*

Silence allows this,
the first wind like whispers in the distance,
like traffic, the gradual rushing
through the field corn. Startled,

we look up into nothing,

the hawk's shriek as it darts
toward the next field,
embraced by afternoon light.

You pull potatoes and toss them
one at a time into a pile,
our winter's dinners spread out on the grass.

I pull cornstalks, stack
the wheelbarrow, leave the sunflowers
for winter birds.

*

*The spoil of the poor is in your houses,* he says.
*Our flesh is grass*, he says.

*

The garden drenches your feet in its soil.
I taste it on each toe, and the calluses

that harden a little more each day
as you walk your miles barefoot row
by row through broccoli and squash,
peppers and cauliflower, onions and cabbage,

pumpkin and basil, what you can never wash off.
Tiny clumps of humus on my tongue,

bits of dirt in my teeth I chew and swallow.

*

How long will the smell of tomatoes remain on our skins?

*

All the wisdom of the ages
has proclaimed the truth
that one person is a completion
of another.

Now the light
divides this small house in half

and dusk flickers edges
of trees and a flock of geese

script their letter across the sky.

You have given me all of this—
the wind sounding the urge
of its own momentum.

That these words could also be wind
and your body the auburn field corn
rustling, or the one remaining rose,

or the chimes sprinkling their scale,
a dust-like confusion, its ungraspable logic,
the soul articulating its gestures on the air,
something about to be revealed

or is itself a revelation.

                    *

We hardly speak,
except to say how this is a gift,
light fully formed, sky eggshell blue.
We work in this delicacy,
this season of reshuffling, rearranging
our spaces, reading for the danger,

bracing for the forecasts.

The first nip in the air commands us
to stockpile our wood and tuck
hay against the house.

We work hard to believe summer
is a memory, clearing out more rooms

for the past, building additions to store
all the old journals and small humors
and unaccounted for gestures.

Summer lasted one day only.

                    *

Empty the gardens, empty the fields,
the surface of the water, save
for a few burnt leaves blown or still,

save for goldenrod swaying
as if abandoned by its own light.

I want to spill myself inside of you.

If it's all refuse and flaking,
pits and shells, peels and hairs,
crumbs and ashes, if it's all filaments
and dust, rusted edges, threads,
nails, lashes, the bones we leave behind...

Sometimes we're stripped clean
like the fieldcorn in the wind's desire.

                    Sometimes
we would briefly die
out of our bodies like milkweed
floating its white feathers
or nothing at all.

*

The rabbi spreads his arms
over the congregation in benediction:

*We're born and we die.*
*Ashes to ashes. Dust to dust.*

*We were dust before we came.*
*We'll be dust after we leave.*

Later, our child rushes
from her room:

*Papa! Mama!*
*There are people under our bed!*

*And I can't tell if they're coming*
*or going.*

RACCOON

Because our corn stalks were mangled,
some toppled over completely

and the cobs nibbled and hacked
through their fiber sheaths,

and because my wife's father, the expert—
the one who, near eighty, still traps beaver

and hauls them to his pond when he wants
a dam built—examined the barn

and discovered *a peck of poop in there*,
causing my five-year-old daughter

to laugh hysterically and repeat all day
*a peck of poop, a peck of poop*,

and because that same father-in-law
agreed to loan us his hand-built trap,

twice the size of a bread box,
all steel and secure handle, and

because my wife—ever resourceful—
concocted a potion of bait consisting

of matzo—the bread, it turned out,
of its affliction—and peanut butter,

and because when I first tried to lift
the cage with the weight of his body

he hissed and swiped his claws, scraping
the air a few inches from my hand,

and I jumped against the house,
swinging the door back and slamming it

into my wife's face, who in turn
leaped and felled my daughter,

I found myself steering this pacing
beast that would, if it could escape

from the towel-covered cage
in the hatchback of my Subaru, tear

right through my bones before my foot
could reach the gas pedal, before

the bumpy ride down the gravel road
to the game lands could wind through

the morning, before in that confused moment
we could plan better lives for ourselves.

# THE LAST MATZO FACTORY ON
# THE LOWER EAST SIDE

In the back room, two Hispanic kids bop
and listen to rap from the transistor radio
as they scoop the crackers that spit out
from the original oven, a minimum wage
job in a hard time, their motions in rhythm
to the machine's need, their unkosher hands
wearing plastic gloves, their backs hunched
from all-day bending. They crack them in half
and stack them in wire cages electrically
conveyed above their heads through sealed air
into another room to be boxed, priced, shipped,
sold, and eaten because we were brought forth
out of Egypt, thrust out and couldn't tarry,
for seven days eaten and for seven nights
lest we be cut off forever. My father,
at the head of the table, breaks the middle
wafer, reciting *and this is what we ate*
*in the desert*, as we dip our portions into
the horseradish to remind us of our bitter lives.

In the courtyard of the Louvre,
mid-June, the late afternoon light
edging back up the enormous stone
museum, as if reluctantly retreating

to its source, a man, thin, dark,
slouches beside a large-framed
canvas of the Mona Lisa,
an oval opening for the face,

exposing a piece of the palace
behind her. He waits
for a customer to pay ten francs
to insert their own face for a snapshot

and become part of the masterpiece,
a small slice of the eternal.
But the face is everything—
the original inside returns

from her glass case our wide-eyed
stares and flashes and video cameras, drawn,
as we are, like Leonardo, to the enigma.
There's no record of the model.

Some say he painted himself—
the patriarchal self-portrait,
the conventional Jewish God—
as a young woman:

identical proportions of noses
ears, foreheads. Only the mouth
perplexes, his a definite frown,
hers—famous, what distinguishes

the artist's from the model's,
flesh from flesh's creation, what
the crowd jostles to witness,
the animal in its cage, the thing

itself. Now the artist-vendor
sits and smokes, listening
to the clarinetist across the square
soloing Mozart in a circle of pigeons.

He rises and smokes and paces,
shadowed by the mansion
that encloses all that immortality.
If he stands stock-still, he's mistaken

for the clown-faced mime posing
in an all-day posture. He's nodding
in time to the clarinet.
He's smoothing his eyelash.

Lilac in leaf, lettuce
in drained dirt. Mother
teaches child to place seeds

into furrows, to pour
water from the vessel,
to cover them up again,

her introduction to the earth,
her hand taking on the soil
for the first time, different

from the moonlight washing
her body through the window
as she sleeps. We watched

her glowing there
cultivating her secret world
without us.

\*

I think of this child
in a sugar box, one day old,

beside the railroad tracks
outside a city far away

from everything I know.
It's late or early

in the confused texture
of the dark.

She's crying.
Whatever name she was given

is lost in the mystery
of her fading origins. Whatever

parents she knew—blood-
of-her-blood, flesh-of-her-flesh—

have disappeared into the teeming
clutter of pedestrians lifted

above the sidewalks. Soon
a stranger will discover her

and she'll begin her next life.
But for now she's a breath

slowing into an even silence,
a heart tapping against

a bundled blanket, hands
fumbling the stale air, the secret

the world can't guess—

                    *

sometimes we are so full of longing
we'll journey halfway across the world,

the urging of expansion toward
completion, another life in our life,

a pulsing body not resembling our own,
her features formed out of a history

that has nothing to do with ours. Because

we have this love we don't know what
to do with, some restlessness

for someone in our lives, unformed,
this need to be needed, to parent,

as we were parented—

                    *

no accounting how it occurred,

how we drifted toward each other
is a mystery of shifting winds, quality
of light, curious patterns of rain on water.

How it happens is how a dream happens—
you follow a story, then you wake.

A little greed and compassion, dark
forces of need, no more certain than

the firefly's motions across
the half-cut wheat field at dusk.

                    *

*Shouts in a loud voice,* the document says,
and she does, for three days,
until her new mother gradually draws her closer

and closer and on the third day
their cheeks touch and hold
until they flush their private warmth.

*She's consolable,* the mother says,
the gardener who understands
the slow-waiting-out, in our unpredictable

weathers, of her tiny blossoms.
And this child pauses and in the silence
understands, perhaps, a new life possible.

*

At sunset our daughter says:
*Now it's rising in China.*

At sunrise she asserts:
*Now it's setting in China.*

*

First this way towards
the dunes, zigzagging

that way along the waves,

circling around and
back, standing stock-
still, studying

snail, stone, shell,

rushing a trail
of her own sightings,

unfathomable patterns
across a sun-blurred sand—

      loyal to some
quality of moisture
or the way the light stirs—

this seagull, this
shore angel we fail to chase
down,

      this child
we can never capture.

# MRS. TITUS

*Open wide!*
she'd plead, not like a dentist:
*sing!*

So we croaked and crooned
our thin suburban scratches
that disappeared

into her celestial reach,
such a pure soprano
she muted our mumbles

and even the bad boys
considered castration.
Operatic portly, but in our elementary

school fashion we said *fat*
and nicknamed her tit-us
because hers were two pillows,

small hills protruding
out of her always-blue dress.
Curly hair, thick glasses,

round balloon face.
Once a week, a break
from penmanship, spelling bees,

recitation of dates,
show and tell,
our attention was hers.

To hold all that voice
her body needed such heft,
a sphere of sound,

held and measured,
stilling the classroom noise,
holding our tongues dumb.

*Reach down! Deeper!*
*From the diaphragm!*
*The blood! The soul!*

If one of us was so soft
as to be almost silent
she would slide over,

grasp one ear and wiggle,
press her lips deep
into the crevice like a kiss

and bellow as if across
a canyon: *I can't heeear you!*
In spite of ourselves

she roused us—and still,
when my words don't carry,
I feel the grip and clench

of familiar stubby fingers
and the sonorous
urgings of a sweet mouth.

Wearing the cap that says *Linesville Lions*,
face lined with the geology of his life,
he stands the whole long game,

watches number 33 his son
make tackle after tackle,
pride registering as a flick

in an eye or a twitch of a cheek.
And for you who do not know him
you would notice no budge nor stir.

His silence is a deep field
you can walk around in,
a word or phrase the occasional deer

that does not reveal his many orchards
of apples and walnut trees
he spends hours into the dark tending

or the pond he planned for his daughter
that is now filled up with the bass notes of bullfrogs,
or the original grain he conjures out of the old oak.

Once, trapping game in a deep wood,
snow came down in a white out,
all of his markings erased like

before the separation of light and dark
when the world was unformed and mist.
He found himself in an abandoned cemetery,

fenced-in, graves close like a family plot,
each stone beneath the white dust
bearing unbelievably his own name,

as if the other world confirmed that *yes,*
the earth is his home, and that
which sent him forth will see to his return.

# HASIDIM IN NEW SQUARE, NEW YORK HEAR CARP SPEAKING HEBREW

Latest miracle, back of a local fish market:
A carp opened its mouth and declared:
*I am the soul of a dead childless Jew!*
*I was sent to do good deeds on earth!*

It spoke first to its executioner, Louis
Nivelo, one of the non-believers, just
as it was about to be gutted: *The fish*
*is talking!* Nivelo screamed. Zalmen

Rosen, his boss, rushed into the room
and the fish, in the ancient tongue, confirmed—
*Yes, I'm the soul of a departed Jew,*
*come back to relieve your burdens,*

*to heal your sick of heart, to give strength*
*to the weary*—then slid into the fish pile.
Attempts to recover it were fruitless,
one carp looking so much like another,

the way they can slip and slide until lost
among the school. When the workers called,
in their ache to re-affirm, why didn't it respond?
Why didn't it raise its voice out of the heap

of its inarticulate brethren and distinguish itself
again? So it was sold with the rest.
Some believe it was as the parting of the Red Sea,
as the giving of the commandments.

Reports spread: a carp spoke God's word.
The Messiah is coming, such was the rumor.
The local rabbi decreed: to honor this wonder
everyone should not eat carp for a week.

What face did she carry when she slipped out of time?
Did it collapse into itself the way it did after I turned
toward the glass door of the funeral home where she
was mourning her mother? Some of the relatives
thought we were still married, those last few moments
on the hard bench, in front of the coffin, our thighs
brushing, heads bowed inward. But we knew we weren't,
just as we knew on some level of desire that what we shared
is as lasting as wherever the life from that motionless body
went. When we'd make love, in our small summer room
in the center of the country, she'd sing, first the scales,
then the tones her operatic mother taught her, tempering
and releasing her full range, surging into a tremolo.
In the thin light of the funeral home, our legs pressed
against each other's for warmth, blood pulsing
a little. *Our flight time*, she said, *is brief*, the way
birds soar between feedings, quick and flittering pauses
in space. We wanted to ask consequence of the moment.
We held moist hands. And in the silence I didn't hear
her prophecy that seven years would pass before we'd
meet again, and she'd be ashes. May 16th, wearing
her sunset dress, arms crossed, stepping off a chair into
the circumference, a few days before her roses bloomed.
Between 8 and 9 a.m. I was sitting in my new life, under
a quivering ash, reading: *Now we are tied together in grief.*
*No way around the impossible journey.* And: *Did you vanish*
*into an emptying sky?* Even the snow falls in this world.
We're made, I thought, of what the earth and sky are made of.
That morning I didn't long for her. I didn't think of her at all.
A heron landed on the water. Was it her? I read a koan:

*All things return to the one*. I wanted to practice silence.
I wanted to write about the pond's attempt to hold onto its stillness,
the quiet between swallow notes, how the dragonfly returns
to the same reeds, birds to their habitual branches, frogs
asserting their presences from where water turns shadowy
beneath the shore. It was time for discussions with the infinite.
I wanted to make sense of the messages the light sent,
watch the water until it opened, as they say it did once,
and resemble the pages of an enormous book. May 16th.
I packed my journal and an apple. I read this poem:
*no eyes, no ears, no nose, no tongue, no mind.*
So it really was the wind that was embracing me those last
few moments at the funeral home before I turned toward
the glass door and her face, in reflection, collapsed,
and she returned to her mother chanting her name
across the yard for supper, scattering her voice
on the wind, the sudden sound in the dispersed light, calling her home.

Perhaps she came down for the apples,
or was flushed out by the saws powering
the far woods, or was simply lost,
or was crossing one open space for another.

She was a figure approaching, a presence
outside a kitchen window, framed
by the leafless apple trees, the stiff blueberry bushes,
the after-harvest corn, the just-before-rain sky,

a shape only narrow bones could hold,
turning its full face upward, head tilted
to one side, as if to speak.

I want my life back.

Morning settles around her like a silver coat.
Rustling branches, hooves in flight.

# MY SCRIPTURES

*1*

You are my Torah and Talmud,
my written and oral testaments.

I perform my *midrash*
all over your body, dusk into dark—

rain constant on the slate roof.
Our love is the small text

inside a circle of commentaries,
each stroke of the thigh a passage

interpreted by Rashi, consulted
by the rabbis for thousands of years.

*2*

Our bodies are the Torah scrolls
rolled together

and the congregation rises
when the rabbi lifts us out of the ark

and hoists us above his head
and carries us around the synagogue,

each congregant touching our parchment
with their kissed prayer books.

And the rabbi places us on the lectern
and unscrolls us to the proper

portion of our passage. And the chanting
and our love cries are one.

*Is it well that the dead shall be remembered, and the Ark*
*and Tablets forgotten?*

Yes, Jehuda, I would rather recall
the business cards of my father's
used car lot than the five books

and all their commentaries, the recipe
of my grandmother's *kuchin* than
the kabbalah and its interpretations,

her delicate matzo balls than all
the much-sought-after mystical
masterpieces. I would rather discover

the dandruff of my dead friend's dark
hair than the inscribed stones Moses
bloodied his flesh—twice—to attain.

Because I'm nothing without them,
whose words accent my speech,
whose motions choreograph my gestures—

dreamstuff are my dead, demanding
my devotion—yes, Jehuda,
it is well they shall be remembered,

their names the undertone whenever
my own name is called, their ghost-souls
more present than this corporeal furniture

of the world which, like the ark and tablets,
hold their form in bodies of beauty
then dissolve, indistinguishable from the dust.

And after we close the book of inquiry,
is our anger a dogwood blossoming?

*

How many times have I died?

How many times have I forgotten
the nuthatch and the way
the light happens gradually,

patches of fog lifting
from the field in enunciated
phrases of happiness? Even

acknowledging the headaches,
the legitimate grievances.

All complaints are confirmed.

How I dramatize
my significant contributions
and plead for my due.

And then a shock of light—

and it's difficult to remember
that my life would come
to nothing, which it did,
as everyone's does.

The enormous bee buzzing
at the window is one devotion,
the swallow another example

of how the prophets
have foretold our lives,
drenched, as they suggested,
in our own springtime.

*

At the funeral,
we took turns shoveling soil
onto the lowered casket. And thus
we bury each other.

So we teach our children, therefore,
what to do with our lives.

*

I walk out into dew and fog,
among the nest-builders, the petal-floaters,

the dandelions as they preach
their silent wisdoms, the full-throated purple

of the lilacs, the chickadee completing
its investigations of the compost pit,

into the empty field whose hay
is neglected, a rejected field,

a field ground birds rise from, where
red-wing blackbirds cross from nest

to foraging to nest—
        nothing to focus the eye,

no obstruction, what you can see
to the other side of, where the wind presides.

My heart can be this field, open, alone,
inhabited by what falls: last snow,

seeds, droppings, body-shapes of deer,
as if it were only a matter of location:

the sun ascending, the willow stoic
in its authority, as if it were a matter

of certainty, the way the air brightens
as the light's emerging,

the morning's mouth opening wider, gaping,
the wind transported from emptiness to emptiness.

        *

Enormous bee, you have survived
all of my attempts to kill you,

sashaying beyond the force
of the hard-covered book I thrust,

flailing it in vain toward the noise
of your ironic buzzing—

a sacred volume, no less, one whose
author never intended as a weapon

but rather as a treatise on poesy, on beauty,
on how love eternal supersedes all

of our petty antagonisms. Now
you pause a few inches from my face,

rubbing your legs in satisfaction,
droning your one continuous song.

                    *

For two weeks running, a cardinal
has been whacking his body back
and forth against our bedroom window.

We wake to the thumping and the red
afterflash of wings. All day he continues
the work of bashing his brains, himself

his own rival, while his kindred sing
out of an obscure nest. There's no sky here,
we want to tell him. We want to tell him

it's we who should be lifting ourselves up
into his world, more vast, full as it is
of the lush new leaves and shadows

of the apple tree. Crazy bird, what
do you want with this house, these
divided hours? What can you possibly

care about our ordinary happiness?

                    *

It's one thing that the woodpecker
continues verbatim the chiseling
speech it left off last year.

And another that the robins are picking up
the threads of their routine dusk
gossip. Even the swallow still swoops

out of the nest it built under the roof,
swooshing across the porch,
stopping our hearts, bits of hay

floating in our hair. Apparently,
the finches, against their better judgment,
still feel the necessity to call

to our attention their yellow trumpets.
And the oriole, who we clearly
offended, has returned, in spite

of itself, to its small red flames.
Why?
Why all these starting overs?

Why not more like us, who settle
our disputes with silence, with never-
speaking-to-you-agains? With casual

avoidances? Why all these make-nice
offerings? Why is spring
forgiving us, once again?

*

June: paradise month, before the hammering heat,
still a breeze, still a stillness one associates vaguely
with the eternal.

And the ancient poet said: *My sweet wild honey
between thy lips.* Suddenly the strawberries.

My children pick them right out of the patch,
pluck them into their watering mouths.

Their beauty is a dream vanishing,
a brush stroke across their thick black hair.

Are the hummingbirds in the columbines
one consolation? Rabbis of the air,

whose lives are you trying to save?

We write to someone's music,
a solitary something in the storied heights,

back at last, after the various struggles,
the body's needs, desire's wheel
revolving around our dailiness.

\*

One in each arm, I hoist my children
so they can peek into the nest
the robins constructed on the porch rafter.

Each morning they survey their eggs
in anticipation of the hatchings.

Is it possible that we can raise
ourselves to the level of these sages?

And how many lives will it take?

And how will this season be recalled,
and by whom?

*from* THE TORAH GARDEN

We would be like the old poets,
who knew nothing but devotion and gratitude,
every word was praise praise praise—

their bodies as the wind, their lives a poverty, their spirits everything,
everything they spoke sang of creation,
their stomachs empty, lips parched, eyes hungry for the text,

the world was nowhere, even in summer,
even as the apples rounded and the quick birds flew
their quick flights from branch to branch,

even as sunlight spread itself, even dusk,
nothing could sway them outside those pages
to which they swayed.

We would be like the old sages—
for whom it was god this and god that,
nothing is as it is, everything is something else
that blue jay, that grass, not blue only, not green only—

move closer, closer to the garden, how it floats under the illuminated
    sky, softer, softer,
into that nameless place—

*be nothing but an ear*, they said.
*Have you made arrangements*, they asked,

in this hour, such as it is,
this hour of ecstasy and service, this document of mid-summer,
these days of drought and resurrection?

We would be like them,
we would turn into the book completely,
we would walk around the garden seven times
out of some obscure longing
we would ask our ancestors to explain.

We would be like the old interpreters,
whose words had wings,
we would climb the lower rungs of the ladder reaching up to the bird's
    nest,

if it weren't for those red raspberries shaped like roses in the sunlight,
if it weren't for the morning sleep and the midday wine and the
    children's talk—

we would be as those scribes,
scribbling our sixteen hours a day, tonguing the sweetness of the letters,
lost happily among the syllables—

if it weren't that we were stuck in the midst of all this beauty,
if it weren't for these children crouched in the apple tree,
faces flushed like apples, voices shrieking like blue jays—

we would know that the Madonna lilies are not Madonna lilies only,
nor are the grapes their blood-purple, not their sweetness only . . .

Will our plantings flower as dust?
Will our tomatoes suffer again their blight?

Or will the corn stalks be as scrolls lifted out of their dwellings,
bearing their fruit as plentiful as words?

We would, we think, be among the blessed,
the unspoken names,
we would be among the stories passed down,

if it weren't that we wanted to sing the whole thing,
the flesh of the earth, the consuming flames.

LOBSTERS

Mickey got me high for the first time
in the woods behind the parking lot
of *The Lobster Pot*, where we worked

our shifts. When customers
thinned out and the manager smoked
and drank at the bar with the waitresses,

we'd reach our hands into the cold
water of the tank, grab the back
of a hard shell, wooden pegs clamping

their claws, and place them on the carpet,
their alien bodies squirming and sliding
off-course, aimless in this strange element,

not like when our huge black cook
in the boiling kitchen would drop them
straight into the boiling water.

*Hotter than hell in here*, she'd shout,
chugging a dripping bottle of Stroh's,
as I lined dirty dish after dirty dish

onto the rack to be conveyed into
the machine, underage and overtime,
paid off the clock. Way past when

I was to call home for a ride, Mickey,
pockmarked, thick black hair greased back,
led me into the after-hour dark

through the few parked cars and into
the darker woods. I thought, toking in
this new freedom, of my parents

waiting by the phone, until we saw
the police cars' headlights slicing
the night like swords, and Mickey

blending in with the blur, and I knew
a hand was lifting me above the impossible-
to-imagine next moment.

# THREE-CARD MONTE

I walked everywhere
on that island, an island myself,
twenty, just up from the Midwest,

ready to begin that long book
called my life, aimless, swayed
by whatever was at hand, strolling

blind. On 5th Avenue—a figure,
emaciated, barely distinguishable
in the skyscraper's shadow,

on the steaming sidewalk,
inside a circle of watchers. Above
his podium cardboard box

he flashed three cards—
two clubs and one heart—
the queen—then turned

them over and the quick slide,
hands gliding like acrobats,
the cards revolving around

and over and under and through
until they lost their shapes,
spinning like blades as if

by some inner force, a fast-
forward choreography.
I couldn't keep my eyes off

what I was sure to be the queen,
the one to watch, certain
if I held her attention

it would prove something
I needed, what I had to master,
this street preacher staring

straight into my eyes,
whispering, voice like gravel:
*a twenty will get you a hundred*—

and I was confident in the heart
I tracked, staked my savings
on what my eyes stalked.

Of course I was wrong.
And I returned to the Midwest
where I had to start again

from scratch, following
in my mind the movement
of those cards and the brilliant

fingers that manipulated them
until they became a blur, like that city
I'm not certain was there at all.

OIL CITY SERENADE

I want to sing to you, Oil City,
home of artist Butch Quinn who is drinking a beer
at midnight and drawing figures on canvas
with cigarette ash—muralist of refrigerators
dumped into the woods, the artist of logs left
by the saw-mill, you'll find him at The Brass Rail
ogling the single mothers back in college,
abused and abandoned, their exes steal their tires
and crosswire their engines: town of despair,
let's paint you gray, let's shimmy on down
to the dollar store where on the racks are the royal robes
worn by every citizen. Let's sing the laid-off song,
the downsize song, the song that says we're going south,
sorry, let's sing the welfare romp. Let's do
Jake's Antiques, the old men behind the counter
sitting on torn leather chairs and smoking, staring
out of the dusty window at the line forming
in front of the Pennsylvania Lottery—one of them
a few years back actually won big, and has been in
and out of jail ever since—let's collect lottery tickets
and beer caps and cigarette butts and the smoke
that floats through the air. Let's open an account
of what we've lost: Quaker State, Continental Can,
Pittsburgh Steel, all of the hospital but the Mental Health Unit,
let's line up all the Prozac pills like coins along
the Petroleum Bridge and offer our naked bodies
to the telemarketing companies and Walmart.
Once we were a city of Rockefellers.
Once we bled our earth of its sweet juices.
Let's walk down to where the water cuts the town

in half, shielded from the sharp beams of Route 8
that glow like searchlights now that dusk seeped
beyond the hills steep as walls pushed back against
boarded-up buildings and dead-end streets.
Smell grease in the air, chemicals floating
like wounded birds from the one refinery left,
and if that goes, we're done.

*

Town with a river through your heart,
you know what they say of you:

*quaker state gone      hospital gone      youth gone*
*charred lungs*
*makes you want to wash your hands*

We, too, are bodies falling apart,
abandoned by our youth,
squeezed dry of our juices.

Who doesn't feel
like your sidewalks buckling
or your vacant buildings
boarded up and contemplating
their own dust?

*

But have you lost yourself
in a late morning fog
for a good while as it breaks
apart slowly above the hills?

Have you smelled the matron
of the Polish Restaurant sweating,

balancing dishes of pierogies
steaming in the sauerkraut air?

Have you heard the soiled smoke
in Kirk Webb's voice
as he slides his lumber-yard fingers
up and down the after-hours strings
of his silver-toned, demonstrating
once again the resurrection
of Robert Johnson?

Has the corner of your eye
caught, in the twilight where
the river forks, a bald eagle
floating into the blurred edges?

Have you heard Evelyn Green,
small gray head under black beret,
shuffling her ninety-five years,
mumbling brilliant remarks
about Zen Buddhism?

Have you dreamed of the synagogue
hovering over the town like a one-winged angel?

Like a floating Talmudic page?

*

It's all the old people,
they say, and it's true,
you see them everywhere,

hobbling across the streets
at the appropriate lights,
staring out windows late,

writing letters to the editor
about the town cannon
and Lord save our hospital.

Saturdays it's bingo and Sundays
it's church, every other Friday
The Belles Lettres Club

with its strawberry cake
and instant coffee.
Their children have vanished

and disappeared south or west
in search of perpetual employment
and a day's worth of clean air.

*

I want to sing to you, Oil City—

The windows of Electralloy Steel
glare out at the black river

meaning the workers are punched in
and the sky will greet travelers

driving in on Route 8 out of Franklin
with handfuls of smoke rising

like gray balloons to the stars
we can no longer see or name.

When the oil executive
out of New York moved in with his wife

she smelled the greasy air
and broke down and cried. But

on a Sunday night, the snow sparkling
like silver coins above the empty blocks,

lights off in the living rooms, you can almost
believe again in the old magical formula

of how oil equals money equals Victorian
mansions equals comfort. The derricks

and other creatures not found in nature
have disappeared into the imaginations

of dead capitalists. All the trees
have shed their soot, the railroad

has rolled up its rails for the night
and we are all working hard in the dark,

dreaming of wind blowing away smoke,
of Orion letting down his sword and belt.

# JOB DESCRIPTION: POET

Isn't it my job to loaf and lean at the table,
to nap at inconvenient hours?
Aren't I getting paid to speak
inappropriately, to remain silent
when pressed, to avoid meetings?
Would you rather me be punctual?
Would you rather me answer the phone?
When the snow arrives, I'm paid
to stick out my tongue. When
the light bulb shatters, my task
is to describe the dark. Don't expect me
to always return to the same chair
like a dog to the same tin bowl
in the corner of the kennel. I sleep
when others are awake, am awake
when others sleep. Hunger
is the most important ingredient
in my diet. When you point
to a plane, I'm staring at the moon.
When you point to the moon,
I'm digging the earth with my teeth.
I'll sign your petition with my epic.
Don't follow me unless you want
to go somewhere else. Don't
be surprised if I respond
to your chastisement
with an embrace. Or if I claim
paradise from my dung heap.
Or if I continue to talk long after
the wind has spoken its last elegy.

# TO A SCIENTIST DYING YOUNG

*for Bruce Terman*

## *1. The Accident*

For the first four hours after
the accident you were John Doe,
anonymous as before our birth,

your great accomplishment unknown—
the discovery of a receptor
and its role in angiogenesis,

the inhibition of which may be
one strategy for treating cancer—
meaning it wasn't in the lexicon until

you found it and became the first
to so identify it, this presence that
arose out of nothing, or, not nothing,

as surely it was there for all to see
if they, like you, simply knew where
to look, like gravity or E=mc2, and

all those other revelations beyond
my conception. Normally shy
and unassuming, you were effusive

explaining your triumph, drawing
diagrams on Starbuck's napkins,
your face glowing with the ardor

of your occupation and, more than
the equations, it's the groping I grasped,
as in poetry, the way in their invisibilities

these words wait for me to find them.
Now you're a body without a name,
removed from your relations,

in that place, perhaps, we return to
in sleep, but deeper, before knowledge,
or where all knowledge resides.

For those first few hours
you were as if under water,
or beyond the most visible star,

where not even your strongest lens
could locate you. Did you make
your greatest discoveries, the cures

to which all of your results
had been leading? What journal
would publish them to the world?

Soon they identified you,
called the appropriate loved ones,
and your death began.


2. *Washing the Body*

I wanted to wash my brother's body,
the way he washed mine, as children,
in the bath, squeaking and splashing,
his older hands soaping my tender skin.

I wanted to touch him one last time,
not the way I brushed his chest
when he lay exposed in his injury,
his breath rising and falling

to the rhythm of the machines—
but rather to anoint with wet cloth
his freckled face, around his blue eyes
and small mouth, to work my way down

the shoulders and chest and stomach,
sponge his thighs and the hairs
we both inherited from our father
and from his father all the way back

to our first hairy father, and so
I am cleansing them, too, if what we are
is some portion of what others leave,
and I wanted, while reciting

from the Song of Songs,
to clean his nails and brush
his hair and recite the prayer
of forgiveness for touching him so,

and to sprinkle holy soil onto his flesh
and place broken pottery on his eyes,
to wrap him in unbleached linen
and place him in the pine container,

readying him for his next experiment.

## 3. To the Woman Who Killed My Brother

When you struck my brother
with your Mercedes, as he was adorned
in running shorts, anointed

in his own sweat—blood pulsing,
heart quickening, breath laboring,
his whole body in motion—early

May morning, blossom season, smell
of lilac—at first I didn't want to know
your name, the color of your eyes,

because I can never know who you were
before this event entered our lives, this
accident, how you turned a corner

at the light and a life was stopped,
as it will stop forever, this death
you will have to live with.

It could happen to anyone. Impossible
to pay complete attention, one slight
distraction—you turn a corner

and a runner listening to music—
classical—on his iPod is sprinting
across the street—early Saturday

May morning, blossom season, smell
of lilac, his whole body in motion—
and we can never take it back,

that moment that changed our lives,
that death you will have to live with.
And the sages say: *A transgression*

*performed with good intention is better*
*than a precept performed with evil intention.*
And they also say: *we should make ourselves*

*holy, and we should be holy*, because
on the day of atonement when we beat
our breasts with our fists for the sins

we have committed knowingly and
the sins we have committed without
thought we do not know who shall live

and who shall die and who shall drive
and who shall be the one driven down—
I say this to you whose name I do not know

and whose anguish I can never imagine.


*4. Twins*

Like one nation divided,
the older—by three minutes—bragged:

*We had a race, and I won.*
The younger would respond:

*We had a fight. I kicked him out.*
Impossible to tell them apart—

in photos, in home movies—
hairy and smooth in equal measures,

matching clothes, thin bodies, freckled,
blue eyes behind black-framed glasses—

as babies, often misidentified—
*David, Bruce, Bruce, David*—

our parents stuck tags on their lapels
to tell which was which.

They had their quarrels,
their little Jacobs and Esaus—

always on opposing teams,
besting each other, one-upping

for the grade, the sweet words,
the larger portion of the meat.

Once, they fought in the living room,
wrestling each other down

onto the carpet, until our grandmother
silenced them in Yiddish.

Mirror images, they studied hard
across from each other at the table

our father built for them—
calculus and biology, future geniuses.

More and more they spoke a language—
equations and higher physics,

cellular receptors and threshold responses—
only they understood, washed

as they were in the same uterus,
as if their embryos emerged

into their original zygote again.
At the hospital, I saw one brother approach

the other, breathless brother, closer,
stroked his chest, laid his hand there,

wept. Across that distance, one said:
*You have been gracious to me.*

The other responded:
*Let what is yours remain yours.*

And in that silence, did they call
each other by their rightful names?


5. *What We Own*

I followed you down the switchback trail of the Grand Canyon and we slept
      in a crevice, and we own that,

and we own those moments tossing the football in front of 4073 Wyncote Road
      until the streetlights snapped on,

and we own the smoke bomb the cops threw at us and a few thousand others
      at the Jefferson Airplane concert, Akron, Ohio, 1972,

and we own the whole country we passed through, all the way to the ocean,
    where we checked into a hotel and you discovered, lying atop Gideon's Bible,

a black film canister's worth of weed and half-a-pack of rolling papers,
    and we smoked it, and it was good, unbelieving of our luck,

which we own, and the lunar landscape surrounding our tent in Big Bend, Texas,
    and the stars, so clear we could read by them, and did,

and we own *The Godfather—Part One*—on the big screen of that packed theater
    in Evanston, Illinois, and we own that fear

when we were lost in the Tennessee woods, into the dark, and you followed
    some analytical instinct until we found—lo and behold—a road,

and Bob Dylan, who was ours, and Joan Baez, who was also ours, singing
    "The Times They Are A-Changing" in the War Memorial,

and watching the Indians—miracles of miracles—beat the New York Yankees
    at Yankee Stadium during the 1995 heatwave—that, too, that victory, was ours,

and I remember how quiet you sometimes were, and I asked about it, and you said
    it's a feeling you get, you don't know how to talk about it, and I'd like to think

we own that feeling—how we bested the myths. We didn't become murderer
    and victim. We didn't cheat on the other's birthright.

Oh, my brother of the other world, my brother who perhaps will greet me
    when I arrive at that place prepared for by our father,

who is now joined by his own flesh and blood, which is not blood, which is not
    flesh, but bones and perhaps spirit,

which we believe in, like the moon, or the unpredictable Cleveland weather,
    or the way the snow descends on the fallen leaves,

or how the sun glazes them now, for their moment, stirred in the slight wind,
    the same wind that blew the Jerusalem dust in our faces, which we own.


## 6. My Brother's Resurrection

It's all about saving a life.
According to *Leviticus 9.16,*
you should not stand aside
while your fellow's blood
is shed, thus says the Lord,

and so Rashi, our interpreter,
reasons: *if a life is in danger,*
*you must save it.* Yet
our law forbids desecration
of the body, and, further,

how can the dead, who
in any case are not obliged
to follow the commandments,
be instructed to save a life?
And, still further, how do we know

if the body is dead, which is,
depending on whom you ask,
when the nose is not breathing
or when the heart is not beating,
which, as anyone can see, his

is, in intensive care
at Hackensack Medical Center—
his chest rising and falling,
his breath surging and receding—
not, it is true, according

to death's strict definition:
"cessation of *spontaneous* respiration,"
but, rather, to the rhythm of the machines,
a prognosis this scientist, this Einstein,
would understand: "Brain-death,"

the experts said, the skull severed,
prohibiting the blood flow and
the organs to operate on their own.
I brushed the hairy chest
he inherited from our father, our

father, whom he had already joined
in the feast, even as my hand
held his hand, even as I listened
to his heart beating with the hope
he'd wake and stand and dress

and walk out of this place into
a morning mysterious as where,
in fact, he already was, not,
it appears, like Lazarus, who, too,
was a brother. If I had been there,

would he have died? Did someone say:
*This illness is not to end in death?*
That your brother will rise again?

Because aren't there twelve hours
of daylight? We, too, were weeping.

We, too, were moved to indignation
and distress. I said: *Brother,*
*come forth.* Yes, he was wrapped
in bandages and a cloth. *Come forth.*
Let's walk out of this hell.

There's a Jewish Delicatessen—
corned beef on rye bread,
onion rings and black cherry soda—
and you do, you rise, all three of you,
and, though you are in the other world,

it's you—a sixty-year old widow
with your kidney, a forty-year old trucker
with your liver, and your heart, that
sweetness—in a sixty-six-year-old
grandmother—you, all of you, lift yourselves

out of your graves and walk out.
And your mind? How it probed
in your lab at the medical college?
Isn't that, too, still alive, in the way
the mind's discoveries are fueled by

and fuel other minds, passed-on torches
in the greater Mind's examinations
for solutions? That's what science is,
you taught me, a faith, and whoever believes,
you said with your life, saves the world.

## 7. *Speaking to the Woman With My Brother's Heart*

Here you are again, brother,
right in front of me, the most
essential part of you, your heart,

now carried by a sixty-six-year-old
grandmother grateful for your death,
I would say, but it would be wrong,

she even apologized, though
unnecessarily, that for her to live,
you had to die, and I told her

you wouldn't die for anyone,
but I'm not sure that's true,
and what you taught us,

through your life, that a heart
is a transferable thing, body
to body, if we believe, as you

believed, in the mind's miracles,
in the way step by step we discover
that of which we are capable:

to give life where there is no life,
and to speak from the heart
is to speak from the source of

what is and isn't yours, or ours.
Will she allow me to place
my hand on her chest so that

I can feel your familiar pulsing?
And, further, will she consent
to my request to snuggle my ear

against her breast so that I can close
my eyes and imagine the way
I'd hear your steady rhythm

as we lay beside each other
in that small room another life ago?
And, in that dark, will you live again?

# MATING SEASON

In the partial light of a Sabbath dusk,
according to the wisdom of the ages,
desire flushes our flesh the color the sky is
beyond Hidden Pond.

Toward the marsh
we creep, the chorusing tree peepers,

invisible slivers of sound and sex—

and the red-winged blackbird perched
on a reed-tip, singing to its significant other
cruising a cluster of cattails.

A blue goose directs its three-note honk
toward a specific section of sky
and suddenly its mate shapes itself out of the distance,

long neck like a taut chord pulling
down toward the surface, wings stretched stiff and skidding
in a flutter of water.

Season of budding,
of gathering insects in evening mist,
of deer trails disappearing through trees
like feathers floating from a great white bird,

the hermit thrush, the woodcock blasting out
of its tall grasses in a sudden rush and screech,

its needled beak spiraling across the sky towards courtship,
wings whistling—

our yearly pilgrimage to the new season,
the pussy willows you said
your father would gather for your mother,

his message to signal spring's arrival.

Once, after they thought all you children
were in a deep sleep, they snuck off
through the dark woods and down the slope
to the famous swimming hole of Hickory Creek.

They skinnied down to their essential selves
and baptized each other beneath the loud stars.

That's the kind of story that stays with you,
half-a-century later. You will recite it
to our children, hoping they will recite it
to theirs. It's about magic, I guess,

and how a certain kind of love sinks
down, immerses itself, and rises up again.

# SPEAKING OF MIRACLES

*for Mary Lou Brunner and Richard Steigerwald*

Rick's wife is dying of cancer.
He's gardening at twilight, scraping
the weeds, telling me about the frog's
calm stare. He says: *The doctor told me:*

*incurable, and I said now tell me*
*about a miracle.* Rick continues: *Enough already.*
*We have an addition to build. We have*
*a fence to mend.* Staring into the garden

bursting with growth. *Hoeing corn*
*is healing,* he says, working the soil,
his gestures filled with their future feast,
staying alive in the single moment.

Perhaps it's a mistake to think
we have a home, even as we work
in the perennial dusk, even as
our children dress like princesses

and prance around the porch. Perhaps
it's wrong to think of the moment
as ours, the soft after-rain of air,
the sweetness of the Madonna lilies,

the sleep our bodies ease themselves
into, the dreams we trust to the dark—
maybe it's our failure all along,
how the tomatoes will taste

in August, and the corn, our error,
and, again, that harvest, our desire,
where we've hidden all that
accumulation, all that seasonal drift,

all that pulsing of the earth,
our soil seasoned with ancestral bones.
In this blessing we call time, we speak
of the blue moon and flight,

of lips sweet as grape's blood,
wind in our voices. We speak
of this fleeting world, inadequate
to the moment, of fresh pesto

from just-picked basil, mixed
with garlic, asiago cheese, pine nuts,
close as we come to eating the earth directly,
taste of soil and last night's rain.

He says: *if there's a miracle, let it be now.*

Two men are cutting the dead tree down,
limbs and branches first, then the trunk
in sections, all the pieces scattered in piles
on the ground out of which it grew.

It's been released from its enormous weight.
It's given us this gift of a new view—
now the hidden church and the woods
across the road can stare back at us

through where it stood and labored hard
to guard our privacy. The regions
of sky the branches divided have merged
back again into their indistinct whole.

All the nests have come crashing down.
No longer will we hear birdsong
from that particular quarter: it will not
serve as orientation or point of discussion.

We remark about the extra light,
the new distance its absence
will afford, the extra breezes
traveling through the opened gate.

Death is a way of allowing us to see
beyond where the body formally stood.
But we have come to love that body
more than the space revealed behind it.

All winter long we'll hack the remnants
even smaller so they'll fit our stove,
warming us in its next life. When
it says farewell, it will be as smoke on the air.

# MY MOTHER ARGUES WITH ECCLESIASTES

At the Wailing Wall, when she danced
with the dancers—that was her time,
that was her place—she ate and drank

and enjoyed all the good of her labor—
and now, her body struggling each breath
under the purple comforter,

her right hand holding the white sheet,
her mouth slightly open,
her pale cheeks sunken,

her pink gown open at the breasts,
her eyes, delicate as moth wings, closed—
this almost-death-mask,

these last living moments—is it true,
as it comes to pass, that all,
as it says, is emptiness, these words, this effort?—

loving all, trusting few, always having
something in reserve: if she had one,
she needed two, she'd say,

if she had two, she needed three,
the way she wouldn't trust the banks,
a little of her fortune in each,

or her sons, a little of her wisdom
for each, not all for one, not the whole
in one heart, in case it breaks,

and you're left, she'd say, with nothing.
And here I am, a good son,
or trying to be, at her bedside,

reading to her through her Alzheimer's
and her stone-deafness and her dying,
from Ecclesiastes, who she interrupts

with her characteristic *chutzpah*:
*No, you schlemiel!* she shouts,
*the day of death is <u>not</u> better than the day of birth!*

*Are you meshuggah?!* she continues,
embarrassing me in front of this wise preacher:
*The house of mourning is <u>not</u> greater*

*than the house of feasting!*
*Have you ever had children?*
*Have you ever had the blintzes at Corky and Lenny's?*

*Have you ever heard Jerry Vale's 'O Sole Mio'?*
*Have you ever drunk four cups of wine on Passover?*
*Eat, drink and be merry—there we can agree,*

yet with this breath that came to my bones
in her womb I continue to read to her:
*Sorrow is better than laughter,*

and I know she's ready to sue him,
she's asking for his name and number
in this, the beginning of her ending,

under the purple comforter.
*One generation passeth away,* I continue:
*there is no remembrance of former things;*

*neither shall there be any remembrance*
*of things to come*, and my mother rises
again to *kvetch: Is this man a putz?*

*Is he blind? Is he not*—pointing to me—
*my afterlife?* Her breath is slowing now,
the nurse applying delicately the morphine,

yet she continues: *Can't you see the bone*
*of my bone? The flesh of my flesh?*
And so will I in fact carry her

with me all the days of my life?
And what will she carry, empty of her body,
the air her sanctuary? Afternoons

we'd nap together, the shade drawn
against the sharp light, and we'd play the game
of who-falls-asleep-first, her assuring

breath, inhaling time, exhaling chance,
under the purple comforter,
arguing with Ecclesiastes, from beginning to end.

# AT AUSCHWITZ-BIRKENAU

> "To write poetry after Auschwitz is barbaric."
>
> —Theodor Adorno

No poetry in the railroad track
that starts at the welcome center
and ends at the crematorium,

in the barbed wire sectioning off
the tall grasses of flowering mustard
and clover and violets—nothing

planted, everything wild, nothing touched,
everything as it was, chimneys
without their barracks, red-brick stacks

rising out of the earth as if to filter smoke
from a fire raging from underground,
the mid-summer, mid-afternoon sun blazing

as if it could torch this all away. No
poetry in the one barrack still intact,
displaying the date of its construction:

*1942*, the pine two-by-fours nailed
at right angles, the rows of holes dug
into the floor for toilets, the dark odors

and the dust-swirls, the laser-beams of light
shafting through the narrow slats,
the claustrophobic triple-decker beds,

the dirt floors, the rats carrying
the diseases, the Polish words
scrawled on the cracked concrete:

*Keep clean. No talking.* No poetry
in the central yard across which husbands
and wives would search through

the barbed wire for each other's eyes.
None. Or in the monument to the victims,
boulders falling onto each other, plaques

in fifty languages bearing the same message
about how this place is a cry of despair
and a warning. No poetry

in the seventy years that passed
since they were driven out of the cattle cars
and hauled past where I stand now,

close enough to brush my shoulders,
marching through the air
my body now inhabits, filing one

after the another and stepping down
into the large stomach of the crematorium
that was exploded by its inventors

but you can still see the space inside
where they last breathed—no poetry
in the black swamp the chips

of their bones and the ashes of their flesh
ended up in, where I stand now, startled
by the glassy eyes of the green frog

that gazes up at me from the bank,
its crouched body stock-still like
the one my daughter pointed

my attention toward near our pond at home.
We'd pause for the screech and the leap.
This one screeches.

It leaps.
No—it splashes among the blessed shards—
poetry.

*1. Next Year in Jerusalem*

Where was that place?

Was it on the tree-lined street
we drove down Sunday mornings
to look at mansions?

Was it on the basement shelf,
too high for me to reach
to see what was stored there?

Or was it like that horse
that cantered across the white fields
when no one was watching?

Or like the word *death*
I thought about in bed
after my mother whispered the story

and my body shook
and she explained it's a place
we all go?

Would it be next year?

Or perhaps it was like
that diagram she drew
when I asked how I was born:

the man's part,
then the woman's:
*This goes into this.*

When would I understand?
Next year?
In Jerusalem?

On Passover
she gave me a piece
of rock candy to suck on

as we sat through the Seder—
the sugared cherry sweet
on my tongue as we sounded the words:

*Next year in Jerusalem,* mine,
she said, as God commanded,
forever.


2. *Planting Trees*

In Hebrew school,
on the teacher's desk,
the blue and white *tzedakah* box,
its map of the holy land beside the words:
*Your direct link to the land of Israel.*
Between the aleph and the bet
we're told to slip our loose change
into the slot.
We're planting trees.
How many will I own?
A few for my birth,

a few for my manhood,
a few for my marriage,
a few for my death.
A small forest
in a country they say is mine.


## 3. Tourists

We travel past hurriedly, comfortable
in our tourist bus, behind sunglasses
and cameras, curious about the F-15s
making designs in the sky.

But aged men and women kneel face down,
kiss the ground in worship. Secrets
are on their lips and now they can rest
where a promise is kept,

beside the stones of antiquity,
among the ruins of amphitheaters,
along the streets of Jerusalem,
where tear-stained prayers

add another layer to the Wailing Wall,
where orthodox request them to join *minyan*.
We need no reminder that this is no museum,
as orange trees emerge: they ripen

generation upon generation, or look down
on Masada from an advantageous cable-car
where it's easy to imagine 960 Jews
bury themselves with one Torah.

And that last evening in Haifa,
city above the Mediterranean,
a rainbow formed while hail
fell like manna through a halo.


## 4. *Sundown on the Dead Sea*

*You could read a book,* they say,

and it's true, it's like relaxing
on a couch of water,

but I'm reading streaks
the clouds of planes script
across the universal blue.

The hills of Jordan
are flamed gold, then orange.

If I float far enough
in their direction,
the other side of the sea,

I'm warned I'll be shot
by men I don't know

on a surface so still
I can slide to the motions
of my own waves, a water

so pure my wrinkles
will be smoothed

and my sores become skin
again.

      I am buoyed by the salt
that stings if I'm crazy
to duck my head in but

who wouldn't risk
a moment's blindness
to wash the whole body
in the center of the earth?

This is the lowest below
sea level I'll ever be,
even my grave is higher,

and the secret to the healing
powers is all this silence
as I drift, in the oncoming darkness,

toward enemy territory.


*5. For Emal, My Jordanian Student*

Mediterranean among the Midwestern
fair-skinned, you come into my office
from the snow that swirls in pockets,
sit down and say you are sad
because the oranges are not so good,
then you notice the picture of my mother
posing in front of the gold dome of the *Al-Aqsa* Mosque.
*Al-Quds*, you say. *Where my father was born.*

## 6. "Rachel, She Came for the Tanks"

> Rachel Corrie was a 23-year-old peace activist who was killed on March 16th, 2003 when an American-made bulldozer crushed her as she protested the destruction by the Israeli government of an Arab house in the Gaza Strip. Below are fragments from the last emails she sent back home.

from February 7, 2003

*They shot an 8-year-old boy and the children murmur his name.*
*I have a home. I'm allowed to see the ocean.*
*Today I walked on top of rubble where homes once stood.*

*We are all kids curious about other kids.*
*Palestinian kids shot from tanks by Israeli kids.*

from February 27, 2003

*And when the bulldozers come and take out*
*people's vegetable farms and gardens.*
*What is left for people?*

*Tell me if you can think of anything.*
*I can't.*
*I want to dance to Pat Penatar and have boyfriends.*

*This is not what I asked for*
*when I came into the world.*

*This is not what I meant*
*when I looked at Capital Lake and said:*

*"This is the wide world, and I'm coming into it."*

from February 28, 2003

*I slept on the floor next to the youngest daughter, Iman,*
*and we shared all the blankets. I helped the son*
*with his English homework. When I woke up*
*they were watching Gummy Bears dubbed in Arabic.*

*I spend a lot of time writing*
*about the disappointment of discovering,*
*somewhat first-hand,*
*about the degree of evil*
*of which we are still capable.*

From the last email (undated):

*Dear Papa—*

*Let me know if you have any ideas*
*about what I should do for the rest of my life.*

*To make things easier here I utterly retreat*
*into fantasies that I'm in a Hollywood movie or a sitcom*
*staring Michael J. Fox.*

*So feel free to make something up,*
*and I'll play along.*


*7. Shalom is My Middle Name*

What my mother left me with—
the word we should mean
when we say every other word,

the word we want to be more
than a word, the word I carry
tucked between other words,

from my birth to my death,
the word embarrassed
by its public display, preferring

its privacy, perhaps lifting
its first letter then retreating
back into the silence. But

there it is, stamped on my passport,
risking itself each time
it passes through security,

each time it wants to haul
its baggage from one country
to the next. Why, after all

these journeys, does it suddenly
step outside and assert itself,
aware as it is of the separations?

Why—
this hello, this goodbye,
this peace?

# LIKE A BIRD ENTERING THROUGH A WINDOW
# AND LEAVING THROUGH ANOTHER WINDOW

Well, I can tell you the tale of the woodpecker's persistence,
the way we can tell time by its tapping throughout the morning,
with or without us, the only-seen-at-a-certain-angle-of-light
gossamer spinning above that field, sparkling in dew-drench
and fog, signifying the season, that no matter what—freezing
rain, more unexpected snow—we have, despite all deceptions,
this turning, this springing, as the willow with its beads from
last night's rain agrees with whatever the swallows are suggesting,
and I can tell you that today I'd really like to be happy,
and that, because we disappear, we want a singular life,
what with the full day-moon and deep lilacs, the afterworld
to consider, not unlike the robin, unobserved save for the singing,
save for the shadows of its nest, the bits of hay it scatters on the wind,
save for the wind, or the soil we become, which is something. And
I can tell you that there's no telling what our deaths make us do—
sermonizing the air, staring into the ripples, anticipating the frogs—
it takes that much faith, it takes that much courage, wondering
if love is a bird perched on the highest limb of the soul. And
I can tell you how every moment reveals our resurrection, and
to wonder what or who allowed us to witness this fog dispersing,
this water, these geese, this willow, is to wonder why the blue jay
would look back to the branch from which it sprang into flight,
with so much sky ahead, or to speculate on how a tree's shadow
is devoted to the tree, until dark descends and they both disappear
into a larger devotion, that place behind the ribs, where we carry
each person we love for the rest of our lives. And though
we'll never be free of our grief, the fat rhododendron's purple
is still drenched by the rain that woke us into love, how the world
happens, by happenstance or design, that the candle burning

all night and into the morning still burns doubled in the window.
So let me tell you that we're nothing, unless you believe, as I do,
that the soul travels from body to body, and so we must fill that soul
with beauty, and truth, and that as it came in it goes forth, like
a bird entering through a window and leaving through another window,
and that our lives are an allowance for that soul to sing, sweetly, if it can.

# THE TORAH GARDEN

I sound the *shofar* for the New Year
and in this suspended time,
my life is focused in my mouth,
lips on the ram's horn I purchased in Jerusalem,
rending the air with its broken notes,
summoning us to renounce:

*Fashion a kingdom*, it says,

open yourselves up to the only moment there is—
this stillness,
this garden hanging like the last blast of its bellowing breath.

                    *

Late afternoon on a Saturday,
designated the day of rest
and so this writing is a sin
against the deep powers of silence.

It's difficult to think of transgression
on a day so full of early spring
four ducks splash-landed on the pond
and the daffodils are lifting their bulbs,
announcing their bursting.

No rest for the robins,
who gather their twigs and bits of grass,
none for the lettuce seeds under grow lights—
already thrusting their green spears through soil—
certainly no respite for the laborious pounding of my heart

as I spy you dressing in a circle of sunlight,
your flesh flushed by the love we've just made,
according to some commandment.

*

*The world acquires flavor only when a little*
*of the other world is mingled with it—*

so I borrow Rick's beat-up uninsured rusted-out truck
and shake and bump my way to Watson's horse farm
where Jack the owner barks back his huge Rottweiler
then climbs up into his front loader and gestures
with his tanned left arm out the window for me to follow
toward the small mountain of manure, motioning for me
to back up and I have to force the shift into reverse, Jack
lowering the loader's claw into the steaming pile and lifting it,
smoke curling as if just removed from an oven.  I position
the truck. The black magic rains into the bed—
one, two, three loads, all this junker will hold.
Fiddling with the country dials, I pull out
and onto Scrubgrass Road, hauling our new earth
pulsing with all the ingredients of creation.

*

Like the Torah,
for everything is in it,
we turn and turn and turn over the rocky soil,
haul water from the pond in white buckets,
rake leaves, gather branches, toss hay onto the potatoes—
dank wet earth for them to root down in,
light filtering through the lilacs.

You pick and bite the top of a garlic leaf,
hand it to me, our longings

226

like twigs in the beak of a swallow in flight,
the garden in ascension, blossoms on the strawberries.

\*

Our daughters step off the bus and charge full tilt across
the sweetness of the fresh-seeded hayfield
toward the blossoming dogwood.

Moses had his Sinai and we have the brief life of this dogwood,
which, if it wasn't so alone among the maples and oaks,
if it wasn't so embarrassed by its beauty,
perhaps we wouldn't be so distracted like those two geese racketing up
    the sky—
if the breeze wasn't so soft across the familiar skin of our faces,
if the spring itself wasn't so unreliable in its arrivals and departures,
perhaps something could be said,
something simple could announce itself and the evening
would unfold like any other, useful and dignified,
disappearing into wherever the dogwood leaves disappear into.

Moses had his burning bush and we have our dogwood.
Would he trade his dividing of the great sea for these children,
parting the clover in their abandon?

His slow tongue for their dogwood song?

\*

You do not count on this abundance,
but all winter long you consulted the texts, ordered the seeds,
dusted the grow lights, began again the plotting of what goes where—
every year you hold true to your imagined Eden.

You tilled the soil, planted the seed, weeded and watered,
cultivating your obligations to the earth.

Swallowtails surveyed the tassels.

Wind every-so-often reopened its song.

And the poems I wrote were full of loss, but of loss with grace,
in the shadow of a willow—we were finding our way into a rhythm,
recalling who we were: June, after all,
what you wanted to hold onto,
roses against the redbrick, poppies soft as tissues,
strawberries fully red and hidden in the unmown grasses,
the mock orange spreading its white blossoms over the porch swing—

when the petals drop, the children call them: *warm snowflakes*—

June, season of tomato stakes and tossing straw onto the potatoes,
hard green apples and blueberries and grapes shaping themselves,
the flowering blackberries proliferating along the field's edge—

and, late afternoons, the sun rounding the sky's absolute blue,
the garden layered in shadow,
the children splashing their thin bodies against the heat—

you pause,

hands resting on the handle of your hoe,
the sweat of your body's labor sweetening the air,
and allow yourself the distraction that, perhaps, yes:
it's all one continuous blossoming,
these cells that everywhere sing their pulsing songs, your life.

       *

And so Tolstoy was wrong:
families are not all happy in the same way.

That the juice packed inside is also ours,
that it will sweeten our tongues until our next language,
the blueberries so abundant we grasp them by the handfuls,
discrete and delicious and without damage,
producing long after we unpin the netting and leave what remains
for the birds that will plunder until they themselves are gone.


Only the frost will stop them now, proliferating until summer itself
     perishes,
according to the instructions of However-Long-the-Light-Lasts.


I eat the fruit of your seeds, torahs in my mouth, dwelling in the
     devouring flame,
in this garden where we allow wildness its portion:


the bat with the injured wing crawling slow as a second hand up the
     spruce,
stuttering one step at a time, pausing high above our heads
and turning, facing us in its ascension:


*Keep yourselves holy, because I am holy.*


        \*


And perhaps the *kabbalah* was right: it's all a tending,
a holding onto lightly, a deeper in,
a flighting and forgetting, a carrying forth, an unfolding.


The rabbi said to his son: *I will give you ten coins if you tell me where
     God is.*
The son replied: *I will give you twenty to tell me where he is not.*


In the wheelbarrow overloaded with weeds?
In the sunflowers drooping? In the apples wormed-through?

Won't we be judged for the pleasures foregone in this life?

Shouldn't we wax elegiac and keep silence in our souls and nothing in
    our pockets,
open to every occasion, measuring our capacity for happiness,
the wren in the willow, the red-winged blackbird in the tip-top of the
    maple, singing:
compost, compost?

*

Among the rotten and the decayed, the spoiled and the decomposing,
where skunk and raccoon feast, among the garden remnants,
the sweet and the stale, the melon rinds and the tomato skins,
all the year's leftovers—bruised apples and torn corn sheaves,
where flies and worms celebrate: I stake my claim,
with shovel and spud bar and post-hole digger, tape-measuring
each hole I've been digging myself down into, two feet under,
below the frost line—here, I'll plant six locust posts:

*four dollars a piece*, Jack Byler said, in the grove behind his house,
between a cornfield and a bean field, all sweat and sawdust,
chain-sawing and hauling them over: *and they'll last seventy years.*

*Locusts posts for the compost bin*, I sang to myself, as we loaded them
    onto the truck.

*

*After we're gone,* you say,
our shadows stretched against the tilled soil,
*we'll push up a tree together.*

*

I want to be a harp for your songs,
wind through the field's tall grasses, shadows of pear trees,

I want to be your instrument of silence as you whistle through your tasks,
in your comings in and in your goings out.

I wish that writing your garden were as easy
as the mourning dove makes it seem,
singing its repetitive five notes with just the right cadence,
pausing before beginning again, a chant
as tedious as the passages of the Torah we train ourselves to recite
     week after week.

And who is the rabbi of the rain,
and who understands his sermon,
and who are the prophets of the wet earth?

                    *

*I will make it a possession for the porcupine,*
or, in our case, the raccoon, who nest in the barn loft,
who are resting now and waiting for the corn's ripening,
who each night avoid the trap with its cracker and peanut butter
and instead tear down the trashcan and scatter its remnants,
and so we retrieve the ancient paint-stained boom box
and extension cord, search through static for a rough music,
antenna directed at the stars, a hip-hop-talk-jive-rap
that will stun these beasts out of the stalks, a battalion
of percussion that will blast them back to their bivouacs,
a barrage of talk and backtalk that will turn them away
from these laborious fruits:
*and so the first-born of the poor shall feed,*
*and the needy shall lie down in safety.*

                    *

According to the laws of soil and rain,
sunlight and luck and the gardener's attention,
all summer long the sunflowers grew,

taller than our heads, taller than our house,
so tall the farmers looked up briefly
from their tractors and manure spreaders,
and we crouched under leaves large as tabletops,
large as living rooms, large as the hearts of saints.

September holds its own,
rustlings and the flushed inevitabilities of desire,
the outer garment of an inner necessity.

Migrating birds, what wisdom?

Speak of the tomatoes' meat and the full moon,
the dance tent, of lips sweet as grapes' blood,
the sauce simmering in the bright kitchen,
our days untucked like the beds we never completely make,

the late afternoon sun gleaming the oak of the Amish table,
the garden melons sliced into crescent moons
and set beside the white hydrangeas.

Our offerings are offerings of fire,
our bodies the bread the earth will eat.

                    *

There's a tree within the tree the light reaches deeper into—

Time for awe and the seasonal decay, for penitents to sway like these
        leaves
in the broken wind, for casting off the withered heart,
for the swallows to float toward the next chronicler, the days equipped
        for flight.

I climb the ladder for the last of the apples,
higher and higher with the thought of cider,

picking each within reach,
stepping out onto the thinnest branches for the difficult ones,
the obscure ones, the ones concealing themselves in their dark clusters
    of leaves—
forgetting the height, how close my death—their devotion,
to blossom and therefore fruit and fall and be part of the larger earth.

Not like Frost, not overtired,
I shake the limbs into the green hail-swirl.
Bella, six and in the flush of her enthusiasms,
chases and gathers and tosses them into the wheelbarrow,
the summer-into-autumn sun perched on the dusk-side of the tree.

It's the day of atonement.
Will we be inscribed in the book?
Will we find a way to live?
Will we have a place to store our griefs?

This is not a synagogue
and we are not beating our breasts,
our sins spread out like this fruit we'll simmer into sauce,
in this harvest we desired.

          *

And so I sound the *shofar* for the New Year,
and in that suspended time,
my life is focused on my mouth,
lips on the ram's horn I purchased in Jerusalem,
rending the air with its broken notes,
summoning us to thin ourselves out, to renounce:

          *

*Fashion a kingdom*, it says.

# ACKNOWLEDGMENTS

*The House of Sages* (1998 and 2005) and *Book of the Unbroken Days* (2005) were published by MAMMOTH books. *Rabbis of the Air* (2007) and *The Torah Garden* (2011) were published by Autumn House Press. Much appreciation to those presses.

My thanks to the editors of the publications in which the following new poems first appeared, sometimes in different form:

*Blue Lyra*: "*Putzing* Around"; "Teaching My Daughter the Mourner's Kaddish."

*The Buffalo News*: "The Summer You Read Proust."

*Chautauqua*: "With My Brother at Walden Pond."

*Connotations Press:* "Abraham's Breaking of the Idols."

*The Cortland Review*: "Don't Ask Spinoza"; "Spring Lexicon."

*Heart Online:* "Our Sacrifice."

*Image*: "Our Royalty."

*Kestrel*: "I'm the Same Age as James Wright When He Died."

*The Laurel Review*: "Our Portion."

*The Patterson Literary Review*: "At Whitman's House, Camden, New Jersey."

*The Pittsburgh Post-Gazette*: "Forever."

*Tar River Poetry*: "Reading Whitman to a Friend Who Is Dying."

*Tikkun Magazine:* "Drying the Torah"; "Walking to Jerusalem."

*Voices de la Luna*: "Becoming Sohrab Sepehri."

*Zeek Magazine*: "Among the Scribes"; "The Sephardic Poem."

The following poems were published in anthologies, websites, and limited edition chapbooks:

"Our Portion," "Like a Bird Entering Through a Window and Leaving Through Another Window," and "From the Book of Summer" appear in the limited edition chapbook, *Like a Bird Entering Through a Window and Leaving Through Another Window*, a collaborative project with artist James Stewart and book designer Susan Frakes (2014).

"Among the Scribes," "Searching for Whitman," "Spring Lexicon," "The Summer You Read Proust," "I'm the Same Age as James Wright When He Died," "Gardener, Whistling," "On the 23rd Anniversary of My Father's Passing . . . ," and "Don't Ask Spinoza," appear in the limited edition chapbook, *Among the Scribes*, Jamie Wyatt, ed. (Out and Back Press, 2013).

"The *Shvitz*," "The Used Car Lot" (selections), "Some Days," "Albert Einstein at the Soup Kitchen," "The House of Sages," "The Famous Russian-Jewish Woman Poet Termanovsky," "My Russian-Jewish Grandparents . . . ," "First Day of Spring," and "Book of the Unbroken Days" appear in the limited edition chapbook, *Greatest Hits* (Pudding House Press, 2005).

"The Used Car Lot" (selections), "The *Shvitz*," "Speaking to Be Heard" (as "For Etheridge Knight"), and "What We Pass On" appear in the limited edition chapbook, *What Survives* (Sow's Ear Press, 1993).

"A Response to Yehuda Halevi" appears as a poster in the Pennsylvania Center for the Book Public Poetry Project (http://pabook.libraries.psu.edu/activities/ppp/2009.html).

"Abandoned Oriole Nest" appears in *The Silence Flowering Its Birdsong*, a collaborative project with composer Brent Register, (Jeanne Publications, 2012).

"Albert Einstein at the Soup Kitchen" appears in *99 Poems for the 99 Percent*, Dean Rader, ed. (99: The Press, 2014).

"Becoming Sohrab Sepehri," "Deer Descending," and "Job Description: Poet" appear in *Ila-Magazine: Visual Arts and Phrases* (2014).

"Instructions on Climbing My Father's Garage" appears in *Roots and Flowers: Poets Write About Their Families,* Liz Rosenberg, ed. (Henry Holt and Co., 2001).

"Meditation in Oil City," a section in "Oil City Serenade," appears in *Common Wealth: Contemporary Poets on Pennsylvania*, Marjorie Maddox and Jerry Wemple, eds. (Penn State University Press, 2005).

"Our Royalty" appears in *Poetry Daily*, November 5, 2014.

"The Famous Russian-Jewish Woman Poet Termanovsky" and "Raccoon" appear in *The Bloomsbury Anthology of Contemporary Jewish American Poetry,* Deborah Agor and M.E Silverman, eds. (Bloomsbury Publishing, 2014).

"Teaching My Daughter the Mourner's Kaddish" appears in *Blue Lyra Review: an Anthology of Diverse Voices*, M.E. Silverman, ed. 2015.

"The Used Car Lot," "The *Shvitz*," "Albert Einstein at the Soup Kitchen," and "Alternative Ten Commandments" appear in *The Working Poet II*, Scott Minar, ed. (Mammoth books, 2014).

"What We Own" appears in *The Autumn House Anthology of Contemporary Poetry*, Third Edition. Michael Simms, Giuliana Certo, and Christine Stroud, eds. (Autumn House Press, 2015).

"What We Pass On" appears in *Blood to Remember: American Poets on the Holocaust*. Charles Fishman, ed. (Time Being Books, 2007).

"With My Brother at Walden Pond" and "Speaking of Miracles" appear in *Enskyment: An Anthology of Poetry Online,* Dan Masterson, ed.

Appreciations: The Termans and Hoods (for their inspirations); Carl Dennis, Wayne Dodd, George Looney, Scott Minar, Stanley Plumly, Judy Rock, Richard St. John, and David Swerdow (for their generous suggestions); Chiquita Babb, Chana Bloch, David Citino, Jim Daniels, Brian Engel, Marty Forchheimer, Diana Hume George, Stan Green, T. R. Hummer, Al Maginnes, John Miller, Ann Pancake, Joseph Parisi, Dan Roche, Saleh Razouk, James Simon, Tony Vallone, and Clarion University (for their poetic support through the years); Mark DeWalt and Brent Register (for their music); Autumn House Press, especially Michael Simms (for his faith in the power of poetry), and my stellar editor, Christine Stroud (for her always helpful and kind advice).

Infinite gratitude to Ganya, whose spirit and support are beyond measure.

**Philip Terman** is the author of four books of poetry and four limited
edition chapbooks. His poems have appeared in several journals and
anthologies, including *Poetry Magazine, The Kenyon Review, The Georgia
Review, The Forward, Tikkun, The Sun Magazine, 99 Poems for the 99
Percent,* and *The Bloomsbury Anthology of Contemporary Jewish American
Poetry*. He has received the Anna Davidson Rosenberg Award for Poetry
on the Jewish Experience, the Kenneth Patchen Award, and the Sow's
Ear Prize. He's a professor of English at Clarion University, where he
directs the Spoken Art Reading Series. Terman also co-directs the Chau-
tauqua Writers' Festival, and is the coordinator of The Bridge Literary
Arts Center in Franklin, PA. He has collaborated with musicians and
visual artists and, on occasion, performs his poetry with the jazz band
The Barkeyville Triangle. Terman lives with his family in a one room
schoolhouse outside of Grove City, PA.

## DESIGN AND PRODUCTION

Text and cover design: Chiquita Babb

Cover photograph: Detail from the mosaic "Moon Musicians"
by James Simon

Author photograph: MiMi Terman

This book was typeset in Granjon, a typeface designed in 1928 by
George Jones for Linotype & Machinery. The design was based on the
work of two sixteenth-century type designers: the roman letters on
Claude Garamont's (1500–1561) late Texte roman font; the italics on a
face created by Robert Granjon (1513–1589). To avoid confusion with
the Garamond romans based on the work of Jannon, Linotype named
the typeface for Granjon.

During his lifetime, while working primarily as an itinerant punch
cutter, Granjon created nine typefaces, including Civilité and Paragone
Greque; and designed about fifty different alphabets for which he cut
approximately six thousand punches. He is best known for his saucy and
beautiful italic fonts.